TY OF
RPTON

e shown above.
d late.
ounter.   (L2)

The Neo-Nazis and German Unification

NEO-NAZI VIOLENCE
IN
UNIFIED GERMANY
1990-1995

FLENSBURG

LUEBECK
MOELLN

SAAL

SCHWERIN

HAMBURG
BUXTEHUDE

SACHSENHAUSEN
NEURUPPIN
BERLIN
POTSDAM

FRANKFURT AM ODER

MAGDEBURG

COTTBUS

HOYERSWERDA

WUPPERTAL
SOLINGEN

HALLE

FLOESSBERG
DRESDEN

BUCHENWALD
STOTTERNHEIM

BAD BREISIG

GRIESHEIM

FULDA

TRIER

IDAR-
OBERSTEIN

WORMS

LUDWIGSHAVEN

MANNHEIM

NURENBERG

STUTTGART

PASSAU

The Neo-Nazis and German Unification

RAND C. LEWIS

PRAEGER

Westport, Connecticut
London

Library of Congress Cataloging-in-Publication Data

Lewis, Rand C.

    The Neo-Nazis and German unification / Rand C. Lewis.
      p. cm.
    Includes bibliographical references and index.
    ISBN 0-275-95638-5 (alk. paper)
    1. Germany—Social conditions—1990- 2. Germany—History–
Unification, 1990. 3. Racism—Germany—History—20th century.
4. Political culture—Germany. 5. Fascism—Germany. 6. Germany–
Ethnic relations. I. Title.
DD290.26.L49 1996
943.087′9—dc20   96–2198

British Library Cataloguing in Publication Data is available.

Library of Congress Catalog Card Number: 96–2198
ISBN: 0-275-95638-5

First published in 1996

Praeger Publishers, 88 Post Road West, Westport, CT 06881
An imprint of Greenwood Publishing Group, Inc.

Printed in the United States of America

The paper used in this book complies with the
Permanent Paper Standard issued by the National
Information Standards Organization (Z39.48–1984).

10 9 8 7 6 5 4 3 2 1

Dedicated to
Catherine, Christopher,
Ron, and Steven

Contents

Illustrations

Preface

Today is October 3, 1995. As I write this preface to *The Neo-Nazis and German Unification*, I find it appropriate to be in Heidelberg, Germany, on such an auspicious date. Five years ago on this day, West Germany and East Germany, formerly the Federal Republic of Germany and the Democratic German Republic, respectively, officially unified into one sovereign nation.

This union proved to be a difficult adjustment for both regions. These two divergent societies shared the same language, but few other commonalities after forty-five years of the Cold War. They merged into one national identity that once again dominates Central Europe. Although melding the two identities into one has been expensive and not always smooth, Germany has, over the five years since unification, been able to strengthen the relationship and bring about some semblance of economic stability. Many supporters claimed that the result attained in a short five years was a modern miracle. The trappings of the past were relegated to history and as a consequence the future bodes well for the unified Germany.

I was fortunate to live and work in Germany both before and after unification. I began my study of the neo-Nazis following my first military tour to Heidelberg in the mid-1980s. At that time, the wall between East and West Germany seemed a permanent fixture. As a unit commander, my responsibility was to prepare for possible Soviet invasion. This, however, did not deter me from getting to know our hosts. I found the Germans to be gracious and, once one was accepted, extremely friendly and congenial. Therefore, it came as somewhat of a shock that there were organized neo-Nazi groups in the immediate Heidelberg area. I began to collect data on these small and, up until that time, fairly innocuous groups.

Upon returning to Germany for another three-year military tour in 1993, I once again was able to follow the fortunes of the now, far more active neo-Nazis. Unification seemed to have opened the doors for the growth of this right-wing extremism, which had become far more vicious and indiscriminate in its activities.

My research for this book deals directly with modern neo-Nazism and the impact that German unification had on this movement. Gathered data revealed that the stresses on German society associated with unification molded the right-wing extremists' often brutal and violent activities during the early 1990s. What is important to note is that neo-Nazis and right-wing extremism in Germany has not been eradicated, nor has it been definitively defeated. The ebb and flow of the neo-Nazi movements seem to defy many common theories, which suggest that economics plays the central role in the emergence and survival of right-wing militancy. What must be considered is the means by which democracies can preclude these groups from continuing to fester on the fringes of the civil population.

Acknowledgments

I would like to take this opportunity to thank the many friends and peers who have inspired and supported me in my efforts to write about the activities and players in the neo-Nazi movement. Most important were Dr. Richard Spence, professor of History at the University of Idaho, and Dr. James Jacob and Dr. Donna Schlagheck, professors of Political Science at Wright State University, all of whom mentored me in this venture, providing valued advice and prodding me along to ensure continued research in this most important topic. A special thank you must be given to those at Duquesne University in Pittsburgh, Pennsylvania, who listened to me endlessly discuss this story, and to Anne Mullin Burnham and the World Affairs Council of Pittsburgh, who gave me the opportunity to speak about this subject to so many outstanding audiences. Last, but certainly not least, I must thank my wife, Judy, for her patience and understanding while I spend endless hours reading, researching, and writing about the infamous neo-Nazis.

Confiscated neo-Nazi material following a police raid near Frankfurt. Courtesy of Associated Press

1

Unification

It is not easy for a society accustomed to little opportunity and risk to enter a new phase of great opportunity but also great risk.
—Ruediger Pohl, Director, Institute for Economic Research, "Still Divided," *The Stars and Stripes,* October 9, 1995

Germany suffered the trauma of losing two wars in the twentieth century, and carried the resulting wounds into the rebuilding years following the collapse of the Third Reich. Modern written histories, particularly those covering the first forty-five years of the century, tended to be harsh judges of German activities during the two world wars. The Third Reich became the epitome of the barbarity of man, leaving Germany with a legacy that was difficult to overcome. Memories of depression, economic disaster, starvation, unemployment, fear, and the responsibility for two devastating wars in Central Europe seemed insurmountable for many Germans. In the western states of Germany, rapid rebuilding, economic revitalization, political success, and regional power played key roles in developing a society that could view the future without dwelling on the past. The eastern states, separated from their German roots, were drawn behind an "Iron Curtain" and evolved along almost opposite cultural and societal lines. They appeared to have eradicated their past by becoming a model communist nation.

From 1945 until unification, West Germany moved into an era where the standard of living was one of the highest in the world. Meanwhile, East

Germany became one of the most rabid client states for the Soviet Union and an important military member of the Warsaw Pact. Communism became entrenched among the elite, and many in the West viewed East Germany as the most potent military force in Eastern Europe supporting the Union of Soviet Socialist Republics (U.S.S.R.). East Germany's strategic location and its use of some of the most advanced Soviet equipment made it a natural key ally for the entire Warsaw Pact.

Russian president Mikhail Gorbachev's *Perestroika* and *Glasnost* in the late 1980s set the stage for the collapse of Soviet Russia's hegemony in Eastern Europe and the eventual splitting off of client nations, beginning with Poland and closely followed by Czechoslovakia and Hungary. East Germany, officially called the German Democratic Republic (DDR or GDR), watched the dissolution of the communist system in eastern Europe with a sense of foreboding and discomfort.

The GDR soon found itself isolated among the nations moving away from communism and dependency on the U.S.S.R. and moving towards western democratic systems. Eric Honecker, the unchallenged leader of the GDR, took a hard line against change. His country was the most dependent on the U.S.S.R., particularly economically. Honecker was not willing to loosen his hold on the East German government or on his people. As the pressure for change began to build in East Germany, Honecker looked to the East and Mikhail Gorbachev to support the communist German government. This, however, proved to be a fatal mistake. Gorbachev refused to provide Soviet troops to conduct internal repressive missions against East German citizens, who were pushing for reform. In fact, Gorbachev saw Honecker as a potential liability to peaceful change in the region, and supported younger leaders such as Egon Krenz and Günter Schabowski. These men, Gorbachev felt, could better meet the challenges that all states in the former communist bloc were facing.

The East Germans themselves had mixed feelings. Communism under Honecker had not been ideal. Many felt that the "Wall," the physical separation between the East and the West, had played a role in developing a psychological division in the hearts of the people. Families literally were split apart in 1961 when the wall was constructed between East and West Berlin. The growing disparity between the two Germanies was apparent when Willy Brandt's "Ostpolitik" (during 1969 and 1970) opened the borders ever so slightly and allowed television to provide the East Germans insight into western affluence. Poland's movement toward democracy showed a way of breaking from the old and evolving into a new system. This option seemed to be more difficult for the East Germans to emulate, primarily because of historical ill-feelings between Poles and Germans.

Hungary provided a key impetus for the revolution in East Germany. Hungary's borders were opened to Austria, providing a means for adventurous East Germans to escape to the West. As a popular vacation place for many GDR citizens, Hungary became a mecca for asylum seekers wanting to leave Honecker's Germany. Many of these people were the young intellectuals who could afford the trip to Hungary and who saw opportunity in the West. The border opening caused a hemorrhage of East Germans.

On October 8, 1989, Gorbachev concluded a visit to East Germany by refusing to use force to support Honecker's government, which presumably would stem the tide of change. The following day, October 9, 1989, a large demonstration was planned to support liberalization similar to what Gorbachev was pursuing in the U.S.S.R. Honecker placed the police and paramilitary units on alert to clear the demonstration areas by force, if necessary. Approximately 70,000 people gathered for the demonstration in the streets of East Berlin. The government forces took no action because of the sheer number of participants and their peaceful approach. This was the beginning of the end. Honecker had lost his support from his superiors in Moscow, had failed to control the growth of influences supporting change, and was shown to be impotent at the most critical time, when the demonstrators took command. Honecker was replaced nine days later by Egon Krenz, who was head of security and one of Gorbachev's choices. Krenz, however, was at a distinct disadvantage. The revolution had already begun. The people acted at the demonstrations and the Communist Party reacted, losing control rapidly. The power then began to emanate from the streets in a nonviolent explosion of pent-up desire for change.

Years of political and economic lies, stagnation, Soviet military occupation, police violence, and the psychological division caused by the wall between the East and the West did not lead to a violent revolution, but an effective peaceful one. This was the first peaceful revolution in German history.[1] The initial stages of change were only the beginning of a long and arduous re-evaluation of socialism and the German tradition.

On November 9, 1989, the Berlin Wall, the most obvious divisor within Germany since 1961, began to be dismantled. Prior to this event, unification had not been the primary objective that the leaders of the peaceful revolution were touting. Many of the intellectuals and leaders of the movement were caught off-guard by the wave of popular demand for unification that seemed to be linked to the "fall of the Wall." Instead of chanting the familiar *"wir sind das Volk,"* meaning "we are the people," the crowds began shouting *"wir sind ein Volk,"* which translates as, "we are one nation."

The first free elections in East Germany were held on March 18, 1990. The people chose the Christian Democratic Union (CDU) over the Socialist German

Party (SPD) by a 40.9 percent to 21.8 percent margin. In essence, this was a vote for Chancellor Kohl and for the fast track to unification. This election was the turning point for the issue of unification. It closed the door on the revolution and opened the period of formal negotiations for unification of two democratically elected governments of the two postwar Germanies.

The newly re-elected West German chancellor viewed German unification as a historical opportunity that provided an excellent probability of political gain for his party in both the East and the West. Kohl envisioned a nation of commonality drawn together as a single national image in the center of Europe. The events in East Germany provided this opportunity. By using the wealth and prestige of West Germany, he hoped to draw the eastern *Länder*, or states, into a common front of equality and economic stability, thereby insuring a truly Germanic nation that provided a stalwart democracy in Central Europe.

TABLE 1.1
International Opinion of German Unification

United States	61% Favored	13% Rejected
Italy	78% Favored	NA
Spain	73% Favored	NA
France	68% Favored	NA
Great Britain	61% Favored	NA
U.S.S.R.	51% Favored	NA
Czechoslovakia	58% Favored	NA
Netherlands	52% Favored	NA
Poland	NA	64% Rejected
Denmark	NA	51% Rejected

Although somewhat surprised by the rapidity of change in Central Europe, the western nations provided the much needed support that gave impetus to Chancellor Kohl's unification efforts. The French and British were not ecstatic about unification and continued to fear German power, however, public opinion in these countries did provide a basic foundation for support. In France, sixty-eight percent of a popular poll supported unification and in England approximately sixty-one percent. This then led the respective governments to support Kohl's efforts. This change in attitude was attributed to the euphoria of the apparent failure of Communism and a need for stability in the region. Although somewhat fearsome, a united Germany was viewed as the best option to retain that stability since West Germany had proved itself to be a staunch ally and effective partner during the Cold War. Negotiations between the states indicated that a united Germany would be dominated by that very same western ally. (See Table 1.1.)

The U. S. government considered unification an inevitable end to the Cold War. However, public opinion in the United States tended to reflect British sentiment, with only sixty-one percent in favor and thirteen percent who specifically rejected the idea. This attitude among the American populace did not change the position of the official government policy, which was specific in its support of unification. George Bush, president of the United States, became an advocate of German unification and one of Kohl's most important supporters. Bush's advisors saw this as a key ingredient in insuring stability in Europe and provided support for the need to decrease the U. S. military presence in Germany. The U.S. government saw unification as a chance to decrease the pressure to maintain a large defensive force in Europe, thereby providing an important economic benefit in an era of fiscal constraint. Hence, the Kohl government in Bonn got a willing western ally in its quest for unifying the two German nations.

Eastern Europeans, though not overwhelmingly supportive in the popular opinion polls, saw German unification as an indication of the potential for their own independence. They also recognized that Germany was a stable entity in a region that was strapped with economic problems and, in some cases, failures. The West German economic strength and industrial power was viewed as a positive influence that could support capitalism and economic growth throughout eastern Europe.

Only Poland and Denmark supported a popular opinion that unification of Germany was detrimental and therefore should not be undertaken. The issue of borders and the fact that Germany and Poland had a long history of distrust and violence were still on the minds of many Poles. The Danes, who also suffered under the Third Reich, were also fearful of a united Germany.

Even within Germany, many felt a certain sense of trepidation with the pending unification. Intellectuals and government functionaries in the East saw unification as a potentially disastrous move. They argued that eastern Germany should retain its independence, develop its social programs, and build on the socialist dreams that had failed under the Soviet Union's tutelage. The easterners were anxious about being overwhelmed by the affluent western states and forced to accept western policies. In short, they feared being treated as "second class citizens" in a united Germany, and this plagued the negotiations for unification.

On the other hand, many Germans in the East were interested in the obvious affluence of the West and were tired of the rhetoric of a collapsing communist system that had not provided the comforts of life which were enjoyed in the West. The "Berlin Wall" coming down opened the doors to western wealth and opportunity. The initial perceptions held by many western Germans that easterners would flock to the western regions in search of jobs and a higher standard of living quickly dissipated during the few months prior to actual unification. One day, the wall in Berlin was a barbed-wire, mine-field strewn, patrolled demarcation line that divided a land of German culture and traditions. The following day, these artifacts were breached by East Germans heading west. Their curiosity was soon satisfied as the majority returned to their homes in the East rather than attempt to relocate into an alien society. This did not preclude a sense of euphoria that began to evolve as the realization of the events began to seep into the population both east and west of the Oder River.

A deep sense of nationalism appeared to sweep across Germany on October 3, 1990, the day of official unification of East and West Germany. This was the culmination of over forty-five years of political evolution that started at the end of World War II with the Allies dividing Germany into two separate countries, each developing in far different ways: one under the tutelage of the West and one under the control of the Soviet Union. Even as the wall between East and West Berlin was being constructed in 1961, many Germans on both sides dreamed of the day that the country would be reunited. Joy and hope followed the official unification activities throughout the remaining two months of 1990 and the early days of 1991. It was not until the Spring of 1991 that the euphoria turned to anxiety as the realities of unification became clearer.

The unification of the two Germanies provided numerous problems for Helmut Kohl and the Bonn government, not the least of which were those related to the right-wing interests that were mostly dormant for over forty years. It is true that West Germany experienced right-wing extremist political parties, right-wing rhetoric, and occasional neo-Nazi activities from a number of small and for years seemingly insignificant groups. However, only after unification did Germany see widespread enthusiasm for the extreme right wing on a major scale. Marches by neo-Nazis in cities all over eastern and western Germany, as well as increased terrorism by young people disillusioned by unemployment and government policies that supported immigration of foreigners, drew world-wide attention to the growing rightist movement throughout the German *Länder*.

Differences between the two regions of Germany appeared to become so acute that the problems associated with truly unifying the country seemed impossible.

The West Germans enjoyed one of the highest standards of living in the world. They were paid the highest wages in the industrialized world, and workers only worked an average of 1,499 hours per year as compared to those in the United States who averaged 1,847 hours per year.[2] On the other hand, East Germany was an economic disaster. Having been intimately dependent on the Soviet Union for over forty-five years, the East German economic infrastructure was practically nonexistent. The wall coming down between the East and the West in 1989 provided the opportunity for a flood of workers to move into the more affluent West. Although this major movement never really materialized, many younger people did move west looking for economic opportunity. To a certain extent, unification exacerbated the flow of easterners to the panacea of the West. Unemployment skyrocketed to over fifty percent in eastern Germany during the first year following unification. The western *Länder* began to experience higher unemployment rates, limited housing, and a strain on the treasury and social services as these population shifts occurred. People in the West began to complain about the rising tax burden needed to finance unification.

One result of these problems was the increased popular support for right-wing rhetoric. Since 1989, right-wing conservatives, extremists, and militants had shown a revival in the West. Politically, particularly during the March 1990 elections and then again in the Spring of 1992, right-wing candidates showed surprising strength in Berlin, Frankfurt, Mannheim, Stuttgart, and other cities throughout western Germany. These radical right-wing political forces, coalescing under the old, but reviving National Democratic Party of Germany (NPD), the newly established *Republikaner Partei* (REP), and the evolving German People's Union (GPU), developed platforms that often were reminiscent of the 1920s and 1930s.

Unification accelerated the movement toward the right. The overwhelming costs during the first two years associated with the unification of the two Germanies far outstripped the original estimates of Helmut Kohl's West German government. From March 1990 to March 1991, approximately $60 billion was spent on eastern Germany. This figure rose to over $93 billion in a mere six months.[3] Costs continued to spiral beyond the original estimates, burgeoning up to an annual expenditure of over $120 billion in 1992.[4] Of course these costs had to be apportioned among the employed in the affluent western states. Income taxes in 1991 rose 7.9 percent and the inflation rate climbed to over 4.5 percent, which was almost unheard of in postwar Germany.[5] A feeling of despair began to appear among the German workers in the West. Ursula Möllmann, a secretary at Berlin University, summed up the feelings when she commented to a reporter that "we refuse to pay for the huge mistakes Kohl made in trying to go down as the chancellor of unification."[6] These frustrations were further expressed during the Spring of 1992 as government union workers throughout western Germany conducted the largest strike in postwar Germany and, for the first time in twenty years, government employees used the strike for bargaining. This strike virtually shut down almost all government services, including rail transportation and refuse pickup. This action on the part of government employees epitomized the deep anxieties that existed among Germans concerning the state of the national economy. Although the basis of the strike was for higher salaries, a 9.5 percent increase, there were deeper implications. The strike also showed the division that occurred among the peoples because of the excessive costs associated with unification.

The German population in the eastern states was used to the guarantee of lifetime employment and quickly became disenchanted at being fired in large numbers as the government agency prepared to move the over-manned factories to the market economy. Eastern German economic opportunities were severely curtailed as industry and business in the eastern states began to compete in an open free market. Once guaranteed outlets for their goods through the Soviet Union and the Warsaw Pact, many industries in the eastern states found themselves archaic in their mode of operation, over-staffed, and not production-for-profit oriented. These adjustments forced the closure of the majority of industries or radical realignments under new ownership by western investors and entrepreneurs who saw long-range opportunity, but at a cost of unemployment. The rate of unemployment in the eastern states soared to over fifty percent within the first year and then dropped to fifteen percent in 1992.[7] This caused a tremendous strain on the defunct government support systems and placed increasing pressure on the central government in Bonn.

The sheer weight of the costs associated with unification forced the Kohl government to admit that the wealthier western states would have to carry more of the financial burden. Taxes rose in a country already heavily taxed at the individual level. This raised a political problem for the Christian Democrats, the controlling party in Bonn, who were forced to sell the concept that higher taxes ultimately would be beneficial to a united Germany. This became increasingly more difficult to accomplish, as the standard of living depreciated and a recession developed in a region of Germany that traditionally enjoyed one of the highest levels of individual living in the world for over a decade. On the other hand, the eastern regions of Germany felt the pressures of being the beneficiary of financial support from their richer kin. A sense of tension replaced the initial feelings of excitement between the East and the West that led to a reevaluation of political needs among a growing segment of the German population. This was particularly true of the younger people, who either were entering the job markets or were paying the price of unification through higher personal taxes. This tension resulted in a reaction within the political realm that was felt during the October 1994 elections, where Kohl lost a number of valuable votes and barely won the chancellorship for the next term. In addition, the resultant strain between peoples from the East and the West caused a chasm that would be slow in closing.

Political leaders of the unification, particularly those of Kohl's Christian Democrat Union (CDU), began feeling the pressures of the populace's frustrations. Initially accepted as the architects of a unified Germany, these same politicians began to feel the repercussions of too few improvements in domestic conditions as perceived by both East and West Germans. Not only were the CDU and its sister party in Bavaria, the Christian Socialist Union (CSU), feeling the brunt of the popular displeasure, but both the Socialist Democratic Party (SPD), traditionally the center-left party of Germany, and the Free Democratic Party (FDP), the moderate party, lost favor in the 1994 election.

A major blow to the legitimacy of Kohl's CDU party came with the resignation of Hans-Dietrich Genscher, who had been the foreign minister for eighteen years and was highly regarded in German politics. This, in essence, appeared to both outsiders and political insiders to be a vote of no-confidence for Kohl's domestic and foreign policies. The political impact was felt immediately since Genscher represented the small, but pivotal, Free Democratic Party. This party traditionally provided the conservative Christian Democrats and Christian Socialists (CDU and CSU) the swing vote to remain in power. The SPD hailed Genscher's resignation as the end of Helmut Kohl's tenure as chancellor. Although Kohl did win the 1994 national elections, his position became far more tenuous with the margin of winning dwindling and the failure of the FDP to register enough strength to provide the normal block of support votes. These events created the opportunity for radical groups on both the right and the left to become beneficiaries of electorate dissatisfaction with the traditional parties. The elections of 1994 did show that right-wing political parties were still unable to develop a popular political force, however, in the East, the revised Socialist Party, made up of the remains of the Communist Party, showed surprising strength in the three eastern-most states. The uncertainties of the voters were quickly portrayed in the elections, and very well could have provided the opportunity for the radicals in the future.

On the right, the extremists gravitated to a number of parties that espoused the need for order and protection of German ideals and rights. The revived National Democratic Party of Germany (NPD) and the *Republikaner Partei* (REP) showed surprising strength in local elections in 1989 and during the first two years of unification. Both of these parties continually supported strong, radical, and, in some cases, extremist, right-wing conservative interests. The

NPD had traditionally, since the 1960s, leaned toward right extremist platforms that dealt with unification. This was primarily for nationalist reasons including: anti-foreigner rhetoric, law and order, and support of a more authoritative central government. Although this political party almost became extinct during the 1970s and early 1980s, the revival of German sympathy for many of the party's political positions led to a minor renewal of the NPD as a potentially viable political group in unified Germany.

The *Republikaner Partei*, led by an ex-Waffen SS sergeant, Franz Shönhuber, enjoyed early successes in the Berlin elections of March 1990, when his party's candidates won eleven seats in the Berlin Parliament. Support for this party waned after the early winnings in 1990, but it still retained a formidable following that could take seats in future local elections. Republikaner candidates won eleven percent of the vote in Baden-Württemberg in the March 1992 elections. This, in combination with the right-wing extremist group known as the German People's Union (GPU), referred to by some as neo-Nazi, won six percent of the delegates in the Schleswig-Holstein parliament in March 1992, and indicated the mood of many of the electorate in the western states of Germany.

No longer were the CDU and SPD considered the primary options by many eastern Germans. Harald Ringsdorff, the chairman of the Mecklenburg-Vorpommen Socialist Democratic Union (SDU) political party, which was aligned closely with the SPD, stated that "evidence suggests that one-half the students in eastern schools are turning to right-wing rhetoric."[8]

Known right-wing extremists and neo-Nazis set aside their image of being ruffians and militant radicals to pursue political opportunities during 1993 and 1994. Young extremists such as Thomas Kreyssler of Arnstadt, Thüringen, became politically active. Kreyssler was a young man with a history of neo-Nazi activity that preceded the unification and the fall of the wall. He wore a digital watch that displayed the message "Sieg Heil, Adolf Hitler."[9] Yet, in a political climate of uncertainty, he ran for a seat in the Thüringen parliament. His eight-point program included: order (*ordnung*) and being orderly (*ordentlich*), secure jobs for all Germans, the deportation of all economic refugees and fake asylum seekers, the return of Silesia and Königsberg to Germany from Poland and Russia, and the prevention of European integration into Germany.[10] Each of these elements played on the emotions of many Germans, and rang true for many who still were obsessed with the changes in Germany and those who feared foreign influences. Increasing criminal activity, unemployment, fear of being overrun by foreigners, and the desire to ensure that all Germans were represented fairly in the newly unified Germany were examples of political arguments that many Germans became susceptible to supporting. The simple approach for dealing with these new problems offered by these right-wing political interests was epitomized by Kar-Joachim Kierey, the General Secretary of the Berlin CDU, when he remarked that "there is a growing tendency across Europe toward political simplification, especially toward the right."[11]

The right-wing parties and candidates received approximately fifteen to twenty percent of the votes from the under twenty-five year old electorate in both Schleswig-Holstein and Baden-Württemberg. In addition, those delegates obtained fourteen percent of their votes from those who had never voted before. Obviously, the young and the frustrated lashed out at the established political parties and sought alternatives for improving the lot of Germans in a unified environment.

The disillusionment with existing political parties played directly into the hands of the right-wing extremists. In Berlin during the May 1992 elections, voters turned away from the center-left and center-right parties, SPD and CDU, to support far-right and far-left candidates. Although the turnout was uncommonly low, with only sixty-one percent going to the polls, approximately one-third of the voters voted for the extremist candidates. These indicators provided a frightening picture of the future. Political movements in France, such as Jean Le Pen's right-wing party and the revival of Fascist political power in Italy (with Mussolini's granddaughter, Alessandra, winning a seat in Parliament), all supported the older politicians' fears that fascism was returning to Europe through the new right-wing extremists and neo-Fascist movements.

Austria, traditionally conservative and a "hotbed" of Nazism in the 1930s, also was developing an active right-wing political movement. Jörg Haider, who some journalists referred to as the "Yuppie Fascist," was a forty-two year old politician who led the Freedom Party of Austria. This organization fed on Austrian fears, focusing on the immigration from eastern Europe and the Balkans. Austrians saw the movement of eastern Europeans into their country as diluting their society and an economic disaster that would most probably result in inflation and unemployment. Haider spoke for many Europeans who lost faith in the moderate political parties and were reaching out for someone who would provide direction and insure control over the increasing influx of people into Central Europe.

German unification provided the impetus for change throughout Europe. Xenophobia led many Europeans to the far right. Unification also insured that Germany was now one of the most powerful, if not *the* most powerful, economic forces in the region. With this power, Germany once again carried a great deal of weight in European affairs.

Is right-wing militancy a menace to modern German society and the existing political system? One could suppose that neo-Nazism and fascism may very well be a potential quagmire for democratic nations around the world. Within many countries whose governments are based on democratic principles it became quite apparent over the four years following German unification that a small but virulent and vocal minority in western Europe and North America were impacting those regional societies by espousing the infamous spouting of the defunct Nationalist Socialist Worker's Party of the 1920s through the mid-1940s. Utilizing racist rhetoric and strong-arm tactics, these groups were strongly reminiscent of the Nazis in pre-war Germany. Along with the similarities there were, of course, many differences that were indicative of present political, economic, and societal issues. What was most disturbing was the rise of a movement that once again was predicated upon intimidation, fear, centralized authority, anti-Semitism, and racism. Swept under the rug in the West for years, and forced into the closet by another authoritarian system in the East, this revival of the German past once again blossomed into a fearful aberration of the *Sturmabteilung* (SA) brownshirts and the development of a grass-roots political organization similar to Hitler's National Socialist Worker's Party (NSDAP). Unification of the two Germanies on October 3, 1990 gave this fractured movement known generically as neo-Nazis, a new lease on life, providing fertile fields from which to attract new members and to implant a reason for supporting such radicalism in a proven democracy.

NOTES

1. "The German Revolution," *The New York Review* (December 21, 1989).
2. Karen Breslau, "Germany's Chaotic Spring," *Newsweek* (May 11, 1992), 20.
3. Thomas Keilinger, "East And West: United In Name, Not In Spirit," *World Press Review* (June 1, 1991), 20.
4. Breslau, 20.
5. Ibid.
6. Ibid.
7. Ibid. The fifteen percent figure is somewhat suspect since it tended to include not only full-time, but part-time and retraining programs that provided minimal support to families.
8. "The Shadow of Their Swastika," *U.S. News & World Report* (June 15, 1992), 39.
9. Ibid., 36.
10. Ibid., 38.
11. "Down And Out At The Cabaret," *U.S. News & World Report* (June 1, 1992), 44.

2

Neo-Nazi Roots

At present [1989], the neo-Nazis do not present a major threat, but they do
have a history, albeit short, of using terrorism, which could propel them into a
far more visible arena.

—Rand C. Lewis, *A Nazi Legacy*

The right-wing militant groups in West Germany were actively involved in
illegal activities long before unification of the two Germanies. During the
1980s, neo-Nazis and skinheads perpetrated numerous incidents of terrorism.
Often, these activities were not as readily reported in the news media as those of
the radical left, such as the Red Army Faction, but were just as deadly. Bank
robberies, weapons collections, bombings, and physical assaults became
commonplace as the rightist militants began to exert their ideology on society
throughout Germany. Though not as sophisticated in their terrorist methods as
the left-wing, the militants of the right were prolific activists throughout the
country. Their activities spread a new fear among foreigners and Jews in West
Germany. The government began to take far more serious notice of the growing
openness of these groups and the wanton disregard of the laws that were
becoming weekly events. Officials within the offices of the chancellor
recognized the seriousness of this problem and realized that, for political reasons,
they would have to address the activities of these new Nazis.

Historically, the neo-Nazi movement in Germany was fairly low-keyed until
the late 1970s. Numerous incidents of harassment and destruction of properties

were perpetrated during the twenty-five to thirty years following the war, but the media paid little attention to these apparently isolated acts of criminal behavior. Militant activities generally seemed to be associated with neo-Nazi cliques and were limited to clandestine meetings, a few incidents of anti-Semitic and anti-foreigner harassment, and a nostalgic use of Nazi ideology and memorabilia. The German government banned these neo-Nazi organizations when they stepped beyond the permissible limits of minor infractions and came into direct confrontation with the federal laws dealing with Nazism.

The West German government finally began to accept the fact that there was an active neo-Nazi movement that was potentially dangerous to German democratic principles. It became blatantly obvious that this movement was one that was not willing to remain dormant, and was intent on increasing membership and displaying criminal tendencies to spread their message. Accepting the inevitable, government officials were forced to re-evaluate the actual threat that the right-wing militants posed in the German democracy and to begin to place emphasis on rooting out the rightist elements that were the most dangerous.

Paul Wilkinson, in his book *The New Fascist*, summarized the issue of the growing fascist militancy. He said that the use of terrorism by fascist groups was not a "sign of growing political strength," but instead was a result of the frustration of not being able to "obtain power through politics."[1] This holds true for the neo-Nazis in Germany. For thirty years following World War II, these militant groups remained largely clandestine. The Basic Law of West Germany and the statutes that were enforced by the German Office for the Protection of the Constitution, *Verfassungsschutz*, made it almost impossible for right-wing extremists to support any positions associated with the Nazi Party of the 1930s and 1940s. This, in essence, tended to suppress revisionist Nazism during the first three decades following the war.

The activities of neo-Nazi groups readily became apparent in the early 1980s. Incidents of murder, threats, and open harassment against foreigners became far more frequent. These activities were identified mostly with individuals or small groups, making it appear that there was no coalescing of right-wing militant efforts. The violent acts normally associated with a minimal number of participants were difficult to tie to any specific group or movement. Many neo-Nazi factions seemed to have a certain amount of frustration that was linked to the inability to merge into an effective mass movement. The various neo-Nazi leaders' failure to combine efforts and lead their rank-and-file membership into a common political force seemed to be the major impediment. As long as this lack of unification existed, the neo-Nazis remained impotent as potentially viable political or ideological forces.

The West German government viewed right-wing militants as a very small minority, many of whom committed individual acts of violence and therefore were classified as common criminals. This approach overlooked the fact that these individuals often were actively involved in organizations of like minded radicals who could be formally classified as terrorist groups because of their activities. Government officials, particularly those involved in the judicial system, normally viewed the actions of neo-Nazis or skinheads as individual acts that should be adjudicated under the criminal laws, rather than the laws designed for terrorists. The result of this method was to individualize activities, thereby insuring that connections of the accused to specific neo-Nazi groups were downplayed. This approach tended to decrease the potential for the media to develop a group identity for these militants, thereby hindering the spread of information. This helped fuel the growth of gangs of neo-Nazi or skinhead supporters, because they could effectively remain out of the public notice and still continue to participate in criminal activities.

The government's need to re-evaluate the methods for dealing with the neo-Nazis became far more evident in the mid- to late 1980s; neo-Nazi activities became increasingly more aggressive and overt during this period. Local political leaders became the first officials to adamantly support stronger methods of dealing with the illegal actions of the right-wing militants. By the Fall of 1988, the West German government was advocating the need to treat both right-wing and left-wing terrorism in the same way. Hoping to diffuse the media hype that long was associated with the terrorist group the Red Army Faction, the government recommended that all acts perpetrated by either the left or the right be tried as purely criminal acts, and that equal justice be meted out for all who became involved in the illegal activities previously considered as terrorist in nature.

In the latter years of the past decade, neo-Nazis enjoyed far more media coverage in West Germany than at any time previously. Newspapers in a number of cities and national magazines picked up the stories dealing with neo-Nazi activities, causing an increased amount of consternation within the government and in the population. One redeeming factor of this period was that the more aggressive right-wing radical groups became involved in the political scene and reduced the number of criminal incidents during the last two years of the 1980s.

Led by the best-known neo-Nazi in West Germany, Michael Kühnen, right-wing militants set the precedence for an attempt at achieving political acceptance. Kühnen generally was considered the standard-bearer of the postwar neo-Nazi movement in the western German region. Many considered him to be the most notorious right-wing leader in Europe.[2] This self-proclaimed adherent of the Nazi's past was the most adamant and aggressive of the neo-Nazi leaders. His followers found him to be totally and ruthlessly committed to the right-wing extremist movement.

Michael Kühnen's organization, one of the largest neo-Nazi groups in Germany in the late 1980s, joined with the right-wing extremist political parties, the NPD and REP, in an attempt to develop a right-wing political base in Hessen. Incidents of violence were reduced during this election year as extremists attempted to obtain political support through selected candidates and thereby insure a platform for right-wing ideology.

This change to politics was only temporary. The government's ban of Kühnen's organization just before the elections forced the militants to reconsider their political opportunities. Once again, the most rabid neo-Nazi groups focused on attacks on foreigners, stockpiling weapons, hate literature, and assault. Their history of spreading fear and destruction continued. The ideologists attacked the premise of the North Atlantic Treaty Organization (NATO) and referred to the allied members that were on German soil as "occupiers." They argued that the West German government was weak and ineffective, and that foreign nationals who were living in Germany were having a negative impact on German society. The neo-Nazis who believed these arguments once again resorted to intimidation and harassment, realizing that their impact on domestic politics was extremely limited and that they would continue to be considered interlopers by the political system.

Prior to unification, the primary targets for neo-Nazi militants were foreigners. Alfons Pawelczyk, Hamburg State Minister of Interior during the mid-1980s, referred to neo-Nazi activities as "an effort to increasingly use violence against immigrants and asylum seekers from the Third World countries."[3] Interestingly, during the time period that Pawelczyk was speaking of the potential of neo-Nazis in his region, seventy percent of the population in that area who were polled said that the laws dealing with asylum seekers were far too liberal.[4]

Playing on the popular feelings that the asylum laws were ineffective, the neo-Nazis capitalized on the public opinion, developing a certain popularity for themselves through the use of empathetic rhetoric. At the same time, these groups hid their deeper beliefs from the populace, which included anti-Semitism and anti-government bias. Germanism, the rebirth of latent nationalism, became the watchword for both the right-wing extremists in politics and the militants who remained on the edge of legality.

A respite from neo-Nazi aggression occurred during the late 1980s. A period of rebuilding and re-evaluation of strategies took place among the more influential militant organizations. Acts of violence declined in 1984 and 1985, although numerous threats and cases of harassment continued unabated. These more subtle methods of terrorism, along with the move toward political viability, became the right-wing militants' preferred modus operandi, particularly under Michael Kühnen's leadership. The smoke-screen attempt to portray the right-wing extremists as legitimate was designed to cover the actual ulterior motives and neo-Nazi doctrines that were under the surface of the 1989 elections. The neo-Nazis actually assumed a supporting role for the right-wing political parties by chiming in with their anti-foreigner rhetoric, thereby legitimizing the growing rightist racist attitudes. Neo-Nazi groups under Kühnen and Manfred Roeder, a long-time right-wing extremist who was considered to be one of the elders in German neo-Nazi circles, continued to develop and were nurtured on the fringes of the right-wing political scene. Each time the government attempted to eliminate these groups by banning the organization and imprisoning their leaders, the organization would rebound under a new name and often with more recruits. The political and social timing was excellent, as neo-Nazi rhetoric coincided with a growing public affinity toward the influx of laborers from Turkey and the seemingly endless stream of asylum seekers who were flowing into Germany from the eastern nations and North Africa.

Neo-Nazi organizations were spread throughout western Germany prior to unification. A social science group conducted a poll in 1981 that queried right-wing militants in different regions of western Germany and found that, of the forty-eight percent who did respond, twenty-two percent were located in Hamburg and thirteen percent were located in Kiel.[5] Although these results do not constitute overwhelming support for the thesis that the northern states in West Germany were hotbeds of right-wing militancy, it does show a definite area where there were concentrations of rightists who were vocal enough to respond to the question of membership in neo-Nazi organizations. In addition, the numbers of incidents attributed to right-wing militants during the 1970s and 1980s that were perpetrated in northern Germany suggest that the hard-core groups in this region were especially active. Although the study indicated that only nine percent of the respondents lived in Berlin and under five percent in Düsseldorf, Bonn, and Stuttgart, these percentages do not necessarily equate to the actual numbers of active and passive members of neo-Nazi groups in these areas. This is evidenced by the activities of Michael Kühnen's group in Hessen and Karl Heinz Hoffman's *Wehrsportsgruppen Hoffman* in the vicinity of Nürnberg, Bavaria. Both of these groups were fairly large and were the most active in the 1980s.

It is difficult to ascertain the number of active members who could be referred to as neo-Nazi militants. In 1987, the West German government estimated that there were approximately 2,100 active neo-Nazis.[6] Out of that number, 1,380 individuals were identified as active members of specific neo-Nazi groups;

however, only about 200 were considered to be militants.[7] This small number was derived by using reports that tied specific individuals to illegal activities where they used weapons and explosives. Others who used intimidation, beatings, or were not identified were not counted; therefore, they were only classified as accomplices or merely general members of the separate rightist groups. Interestingly, the government reported that the types of people who generally were involved in the right-wing extremist movement and who could be considered as neo-Nazi sympathizers were from a variety of professions, many of which were associated with the civil service. Reports prepared by the different police agencies that tracked the right-wing radicals indicated that eighty-six officials who held positions of influence in the western *Länder* were known neo-Nazi members.[8] Of these, thirty-three were school teachers, eight were judicial justices, seven were involved in finance, and nine were police officers.[9]

Investigations of federal offices concluded that a number of civil servants and military were probably also members of different neo-Nazi groups or supporters of right-wing extremist interests and activities. These conclusions readily support the theory that the neo-Nazi movement during the 1970s and 1980s was not the sole domain of the unemployed, under-educated, bored youth, but included a portion of the West German population that was responsible for the health and welfare of the Federal Republic. These participants, many of whom remained on the fringes of the neo-Nazi groups, were driven by a sense of duty to support ultra-conservative values and Germany's nationalism. Law and order were considered by this segment of society to be the key to the German future. This tended to be portrayed as the need to strengthen laws that prohibited the dissolution of German values, which included the apparent dilution of Germany's social order by foreigners and asylum seekers. These more sophisticated supporters of neo-Nazism tended to remain in the background of the movement, providing moral support, finances, and a sense of semi-legality to the organizations.

Those that became the "soldiers" were the young and frustrated since they were susceptible to the emotional slogans and facile answers provided by the neo-Nazi leadership, who symbolized authority, support, and stability. In general, these young participants were not ideologically aligned like the more sophisticated government employees, but were searching for a support group that would allay their fears associated with unemployment. A great majority of these younger members were part of the lower blue-collar class that was heavily impacted in a society of eight percent unemployment. As a growing source of membership, this portion of German youth brought with them a fatalist view of the economic situation in Germany and a sense of frustration associated with the inability to obtain meaningful work.

During the latter years of the 1980s, just prior to the Berlin Wall coming down, neo-Nazi membership and activities showed a surprising increase. A government estimate in 1988 indicated a ten percent increase in membership in just one year, from 1987 to 1988.[10] Acts of violence increased during the same period from seventy-one to seventy-six incidents.[11] This period of time was a watershed for right-wing militancy. Political issues dealing with immigration and economics, as well as the rapidly changing environment in the East, put tremendous pressures on West German society. Many young people turned to the neo-Nazi movement to vent their frustrations against a societal system that they perceived to be unable or disinterested in solving the problem of unemployment. The perception that foreigners were receiving more benefits than nationals increased the tension.

The neo-Nazi groups used the 1980s to develop the foundation for the growth of right-wing militancy in unified Germany. In most cases, they quietly perpetuated Nazi ideology and traditions that continued to fester in postwar Germany. For four and one-half decades, a minority remained active in western Germany, supporting such issues as German nationalism, historical revisionism, and anti-democratic principles. The youth of the 1970s and 1980s picked these concepts to base a new nationalism upon. New leaders, such as Michael Kühnen, Christian Worch, Karl Heinz Hoffman, and the Austrian, Gottfried Küssel, led those who felt a growing dissatisfaction with government and foreign influences into a movement that coalesced during the late 1980s into an international front of right-wing militants from throughout continental Europe.

NOTES

1. Paul Wilkerson, *The New Fascists* (London: Grant McIntyre, Ltd., 1981), 103.

2. Ingo Hasselbach, "How Nazis Are Made," *The New Yorker* (January 8, 1996), 42.

3. LEXIS/NEXUS, "Increased Neo-Nazi Violence Against Refugees In West Germany," *Reuter's North European Service* (September 5, 1986).

4. Ibid.

5. Herber Jäger et al., *Lebenslaufanalyses* (Opladen: Westdeutscher Verlag GmbH, 1981), 69.

6. Bundesminister des Innern, *Verfassungsschutzbericht* (Bonn: Graphische Betriebe, 1987), 100.

7. Ibid.

8. Ibid., 99.

9. Ibid.

10. Reuter Summary (May 26, 1988).

11. Ibid.

3

The Pain of Change

Failure to come to terms properly with the German Democratic Republic past
might produce a rightist eruption in years ahead.
—Markus Mengel (SPD Bundestag Deputy),
The Stars and Stripes, August 13, 1993

As was discussed, right-wing militancy, often referred to simply as neo-Nazism,
did not develop suddenly during unification. A long and varied history of neo-
Nazism has been recorded which shows that this new fascism remained on the
fringes of postwar German society from the end of World War II until
unification. Many aging members of the defunct National Socialist Worker's
Party carried the Nazi ideology and fanaticism into the postwar German political
and civil sectors. Later, young Germans who were disadvantaged in the growing
technological revolution in Germany during the 1970s and 1980s sought reasons
for their shortcomings and looked for a means of expressing their dissatisfaction.
Using the *Ausländer* (foreigners) and *Gastarbeiter* (guest workers) as a focal point
for their dissatisfaction, groups of youth throughout the Federal Republic of
Germany began banding together into right-wing organizations, some of which
became extremely violent.

During the 1970s and 1980s, West German right-wing militants were almost
exclusively drawn from the lower classes of German society. Unequipped with
the skills or education to meet the demands of a modern technologically oriented

industrial nation, these young people were excluded from many jobs. Unemployment led to frustration, which then led to the need to justify the reasons for being unable to compete. Naturally, the perception that someone else was taking the jobs provided the opportunity for rightist dissidents to draw the disenchanted together. Using the perception that the people taking away the jobs were foreigners and asylum seekers, particularly Turks, the militant right-wing leaders developed a strong and virulent movement that decried the government's support of foreign workers. The new members brought with them a fatalist view of the economic situation in Germany and a sense of pent-up frustration that then was channeled by the separate neo-Nazi and skinhead leaders.

Militant extremist organizations became far more evident to outsiders during the late 1970s. Groups such as Michael Kühnen's *Aktionsgemeinschaft Nationaler Sozialisten* (ANS), Manfred Roeder's *Deutsche Aktionsgruppe* (DA), and Karl Heinz Hoffman's *Wehrsportgruppen Hoffman* took center stage in Germany as the preeminent neo-Nazi organizations.

During the formative years of the neo-Nazis, many men with wartime Nazi pasts became intimately involved in the rising neo-Nazi movement. Manfred Roeder, leader of the DA in Hamburg, was born in 1929 and spent the years following the fall of Hitler's Reich openly supporting Nazi traditions and furthering neo-Nazi activities. Paul Otte, a primary ideologist for the early movement, was born in 1924 and was a member of the Wehrmacht from 1942 to 1945. Heinrich Eisermann, considered by many to be the elder statesman for neo-Nazi ideology prior to unification, had been a Hitler appointee in Schleswig-Holstein. And last but not least, the well-known Otto-Ernst Remer, born in 1912, was known for his rapid rise in the Nazi military hierarchy following the assassination attempt on Hitler in April 1944. Remer's mercuric move into the higher levels of Hitler's organization was the result of his efforts as the officer in charge of arresting the conspirators in Berlin following the attempt on Hitler's life. He pursued this mission quickly and efficiently. Hitler promoted Remer from army major to full colonel over the telephone and assigned him to command his personal bodyguard. At war's end, Otto Remer had obtained the rank of major general and was a trusted subordinate. Following the war, he was not charged as a war criminal, but in fact was temporarily employed by the U. S. government. During the German denazification program, Remer was forced to flee Germany in 1952 rather than accept imprisonment. He emigrated to Egypt and became a security adviser to Gamal Abdel Nasser. He then became an arms dealer with the Orient Trading Company in Damascas, Syria. In the 1960s, Remer returned to Germany and became an important link for right-wing extremists and middle-eastern contacts. Interestingly, he was a bitter rival of Michael Kühnen. In 1993, Otto Remer fled Germany again after being convicted for denying the Holocaust. He published pamphlets in 1991 and 1992 in which he claimed that the persecution of Jews under the Nazis "was a lie spread by the victorious Allies and Jews to force Germans to pay war reparations." His writings denying the Holocaust continue to be cited by German neo-Nazis. All of these men, Roeder, Otte, Eisermann, and Remer, tied the old Nazi legacy to the new neo-Nazi movement. Each provided their own brand of Nazi ideology and set the stage for the younger generation to use portions of their teachings to develop a new form of Nazism.

The growing neo-Nazi movement found effective leadership during the late 1970s. Michael Kühnen was a former lieutenant in the West German army who was forced to resign because of his political activities. He was the most active and visual force in the growth of neo-Nazism during this period.

Kühnen was born in 1955 into a middle-class, Catholic family. By the time he was fifteen years old, he was politically active, initially being a Maoist. He spent eighteen years as an extremist and ultimately was incarcerated for seven and one-half years of that time. In 1977, he organized his first neo-Nazi organization, which was called *Aktionsgemeinschaft Nationaler Sozialisten* (ANS), National Socialist Common Action Group. Kühnen's reputation developed quickly as he provided journalists with opportunities to photograph him in black knee-high boots and a black shirt with a swastika armband.[1] Throughout his militant career, he projected an image of a clean-cut intellectual. He had "fine, pointed features and wore his black hair cut close and shaved on the sides with a strong part."[2] Kühnen proved to be very charismatic; however, he also tended to be somewhat aloof. His shortcoming in becoming a "new Hitler" was his apparent inability to communicate with the general population within the movement. Those closest to him often thought he was too "intellectual" for the majority of his followers.[3] In essence, Kühnen was far above the average neo-Nazi and was really unable to speak to them on their level. He remained a virtual social outcast and never seemed to profit from his efforts. This, however, did not diminish his position as an undisputed neo-Nazi leader in Germany. Kühnen undoubtedly was the most famous and some say, most feared neo-Nazi leader from the late 1980s until his death in 1991.

The ANS showed its aggressiveness by carrying out a number of arms thefts and robberies in Germany during the late 1970s. Kühnen's overt use of Nazi slogans and the distribution of Nazi propaganda materials placed him at the forefront of the West German neo-Nazi movement. His position was clear: He questioned the need for NATO, attacked the "occupation" of German soil by the western powers, criticized the government for their guest worker policies, and, ironically, initially argued that homosexuality was weakening German society.[4] These open attacks on the foundations of German democratic principles led to

Kühnen's arrest in 1979. He was charged with inciting racial hatred and went on to use the trial as a forum for expounding on his Nationalist Socialist views. Kühnen then was sentenced to a short prison term. After serving the sentence, he left Germany and went to Paris, France, and again organized a neo-Nazi group called the *Aktionsfront Nationaler Sozialisten/Nationale Aktivisten* (ANS/NA), which proved to be an extremely active militant organization until it was banned by the German government in December 1983. In January 1985, Kühnen again was sentenced to prison, this time for three years and four months for disseminating neo-Nazi material in Germany. Although incarcerated, he was able to attract new members for yet another organization called "The Movement." This group actively picked up where the banned ANS-NA had left off in 1983, carrying forward the old programs initiated by Kühnen in his first two attempts. However, in 1986 a split occurred, with some of Kühnen's followers moving toward a more politically oriented program. The new organization was named *Nationale Sammlung* (NS) (National Gathering) and was the primary group that Kühnen supported following his release from prison in late 1988.

With elections coming up in 1989, Kühnen's organization became politically active by supporting right-wing extremist candidates in the West German state of Hessen. Four weeks before the elections, Bundesminister Friedrich Zimmermann (CSU) banned the *Nationale Sammlung*. Police raided the homes of suspected Kühnen supporters and found large amounts of propaganda, pictures of Hitler, swastikas, and a small number of munitions. Once again Michael Kühnen's organization was banned, and he immediately reorganized under a new name, carrying his membership and ideology forward into the new post-Cold War era.

In the East, unification brought with it a new and potentially dangerous phenomenon. East Germany was a rich and fertile region for right-wing extremists to sow their ideology and obtain recruits. Throughout the eastern states, which Communism dominated over for forty-five years, a subculture of die-hard Fascists began to surface after the collapse of the Communist government. These people were often those who were Nazis before the collapse of the Third Reich and then had gone underground during the postwar occupation. In addition, there were those who carried a strong dislike for Communism, but approved of central authority and therefore embraced Fascist ideology. Referred to as "closet Nazis," they carefully withheld their dogma, bowing instead to the dictatorial pressures of East Germany's Communist regime. The dismantling of this regime allowed the latent Nazism to surface, insuring both an active and passive support base for right-wing militants from the West to quickly develop organizations throughout the eastern *Länder*.

Although Michael Kühnen was the primary impetus for the growth of a rabid neo-Nazi movement in West Germany, there were a number of militant groups spread around the country. Manfred Roeder's organization, although small, survived the 1980s, even with Roeder being imprisoned for a majority of that time. He was sentenced in 1982 to thirteen years in prison for his activities, but he was released in February 1990. Numerous groups splintered off from the major organizations during this period, making a number of small and seemingly ineffective cells. The Communist collapse in eastern Germany and the move toward unification provided the opportunity to strengthen these disparate neo-Nazi groups and potentially found common ground for a national movement. Immediately following the fall of the Berlin Wall and the opening of the borders between East and West Germany, Michael Kühnen and his lieutenants moved into the eastern towns looking for support.

One of the most important efforts to organize in eastern Germany was focused in Berlin. Ingo Hasselbach, responding to the recommendations of Kühnen, organized a neo-Nazi political party in East Berlin on February 1, 1990. This organization, referred to as the "National Alternative" (NA), was predicated on a legal application for approval as a political party in the still evolving East German democracy. Although openly Nazi parties were forbidden, the new East German government, headed by Hans Modrow, was overwhelmed by the number of applications. This gave the NA the opportunity to become a recognized political entity with few questions asked.[5]

Kühnen's handpicked leader for the NA, Ingo Hasselbach, came from a background of rebellion and anti-government activities. Ingo was the illegitimate son of a young woman who had an affair with a married man while working with him in an East German press agency. Although the affair lasted less than a year, Ingo's biological father stayed in touch with his ex-lover and her son for twenty years.[6] As Ingo grew up, he knew his father only as an uncle, not learning that this man was actually his father until he was in his teens.

During his early years, Ingo spent much of his time with his grandparents, where he enjoyed some amount of stability. His life changed when his mother married a strict disciplinarian who often beat him. Ingo began spending time on the streets of Berlin, especially with a group of hippies in a local commune. Since he was tall for his age and looked much older than he was, he was able to move around the streets of East Berlin easily.

By the time Ingo Hasselbach was in his teens, he had already developed a reputation as a troublemaker and had spent time in jail. He moved from the hippie stage to the punk scene, where he became adept at stealing and street fighting.

Prison provided the forum for Ingo's move into neo-Nazism. Just prior to the dissolution of the GDR, he was sentenced to a prison term in a facility that housed a number of ex-Nazis. He referred to this experience as a "school that prepared a person for a life in a community without scruples."[7] This environment was an ideal place to acquire the rudiments of Nazism. Old Nazis such as Heinz Barth, referred to as the "Butcher of Oradour," who led the SS extermination in the French town of Oradour, and Henry Schmidt, the Gestapo commissar in charge of Jewish affairs in Dresden, graced the prison grounds and were more than accommodating in explaining their "glorious cause."[8] Both of these Nazis were arrested in the mid-1980s after having lived in the GDR for years without being recognized. In fact, both of these men rose to high levels of responsibility in East Germany prior to being caught and punished for their crimes committed during the Third Reich.

Influenced by such inmates and under the seemingly same system of authority that the Communists claimed was Fascist, many of the young rebels, such as Ingo Hasselbach, began to develop a deep-seated hatred of the anti-Fascist state that used the same methods of punishment and control that were associated with Hitler's Gestapo. Generally, the young "political prisoners" in the GDR did not know much about Nazi ideology, but they tended to admire the resistance of the old Nazis.[9] As an example of this rebellious attitude among the older prisoners, on Hitler's birthday, April 20, 1987, the old adherents of Hitler's Reich painted swastikas on toilet paper and then made arm-bands to be worn in remembrance of their fallen leader.[10] The younger inmates saw parallels between the efforts of the elders and their own attempts to fight against the government.

Initially, when the neo-Nazis and skinheads began to surface in East Germany during the 1980s, the local police ignored these new rebels. However, as the right-wing militants became more aggressive, officials began to use harsh punishments. Instead of eliminating the activities of the new fascists, this action led to increased neo-Nazi and skinhead activity coupled with rapidly growing membership throughout East Germany.

By January 1988, right-wing militants within East Berlin who were not in prison decided to develop a brotherhood, called a *Kameradschaft*, after the old Nazi term. They named this new organization the "Movement of 30th of January," which came from the original date of the Nazi seizure of power in 1933. When the Berlin Wall came down in the Fall of 1989, these "rowdies" were already primed to join the West German neo-Nazi movement. Eastern neo-Nazis did not necessarily think much about what a swastika meant, but they knew that it was the most forbidden of all symbols and therefore was a valuable tool for showing their rebellion.[11]

Kühnen's support of Ingo Hasselbach and his newly organized National Alternative provided the impetus for the rapid growth of neo-Nazism in Berlin.

In the first few months of 1990, the NA grew quickly. It became one of the strongest right-wing extremist parties in Germany. By late 1990, Ingo could count over 800 members, most in their 20s, and a fair number with good jobs, who were prepared to commit to ideological work as well as fighting.[12]

Unintentionally, the police provided one of the best means of recruitment for the NA. In the Spring of 1990, the authorities stormed the National Alternative stronghold in East Berlin. This was in response to a growing battleground in the neighborhood between neo-Nazis and the "Antifa," or anti-Fascists, who were often as brutal and unscrupulous as their nemeses, the members of the NA. The police action actually made the National Alternative famous. Journalists from all over the world wanted to interview the NA members. In response, Ingo charged 200 to 1000 Deutsche Mark for each interview.[13] Most of the collected funds flowed into the party coffers, providing valuable resources for purchasing weapons and strengthening the organization.

Ingo Hasselbach saw the opportunity to pursue other sources of support once the NA gained renown. He started courting West Berlin's Nazi professional elite. Although they remained discreet supporters, they became an invaluable financial source. In addition, he was able to develop contacts among elderly Nazi widows living in the Berlin area. They would gossip about Fred Leuchter's article "The Auschwitz Lie,"[14] distribute Holocaust denial literature, and often worked as agents and spies for the neo-Nazi movement.[15] Interestingly, the police kept these "little old ladies" under surveillance, but shunned imprisoning them because of the potential public response that these women were "just" old ladies who were "harmless."

Recruiting for the NA was based on the goal of making potential members feel that the neo-Nazi way was simple to understand. The idea was to make the recruit feel like he was intelligent and that he would fit easily into a growing circle of good friends who would support him. Inherent in this concept was the argument that each recruit was chosen at birth and that he was biologically superior to others. Therefore, each member could easily grasp the concept of biological superiority, unlike those who were Jewish or "living under American lies."[16]

Associated with recruiting was the development of a localized ideology based on putting hatred in a positive light, often referring to "racism being racial pride."[17] These East German neo-Nazis felt that responsibility for victims being beaten rested with the victims themselves. "They were biologically inferior and therefore brought trouble on themselves by mixing with the master race [sic]."[18] Hasselbach appointed a "race educator" to insure continuity in his members' racial education. Arnulf Priem was a forty year old neo-Nazi who looked more like a Nazi "Rocker" with his long greasy hair than an ideologist for a Fascist organization. He held a degree in business administration and was the head of the *Wotan's Volk* neo-Nazi group. Priem was the undisputed leading source of old Nazi films, which could not be found anywhere else.

The National Alternative neo-Nazi organization, often referred to merely as the "Movement," was intentionally designed to be as decentralized and anonymous as possible. Members then could distance themselves from acts of violence committed in the name of the organization. The ability to use "deniability helped keep the members morally and legally free of guilt."[19] By 1991, the NA had taken this concept to heart and had begun stockpiling weapons, ammunition, and grenades to support their anti-establishment plans. They purchased about twenty bazookas and over 100 machine guns from Russian soldiers in Berlin.[20]

Even regions outside of Berlin began to yield to neo-Nazi activity. Cottbus, a small town near the Polish border, was located in a region that was referred to as the "Nazi Belt." This area proved to be especially susceptible to neo-Nazi influence. Ingo Hasselbach claimed that this region was where "no foreigner was safe, starting at sundown on Friday night."[21]

The development of such an active neo-Nazi movement in the East proved to be an effective effort on the part of Kühnen, providing a fertile area of support for the right-wing rhetoric and militancy that the most active neo-Nazi organizations were able to exploit. The governments of both East and West Germany were unable to control the rapidly growing right-wing movement as more pressing issues dealing with the move to unification seemed to have higher priorities.

Unification gave an immediate surge to the growing right-wing militant movement. In the East, reality quickly replaced euphoria as unemployment and costs skyrocketed within the first six months. Those most affected by unemployment were the blue collar workers, women, and the young. The demise of state-run industries forced thousands out of jobs. The year immediately following unification was especially difficult, with over fifty percent of the population in the eastern states being unemployed or under-employed. Although during subsequent years this number radically declined, by 1994 the percentage of unemployed in the East still was hovering around fifteen percent. The younger worker, eighteen to twenty-five years of age, was still the beneficiary of the high rate of unemployment, particularly those who were destined to work in semi-skilled jobs. Many people were literally overwhelmed with the rapidity of change as industries closed, workers were laid off, and commodity costs inflated beyond reach for the average person. A feeling of fear and discouragement permeated many regions of the eastern *Länder*, providing fertile grounds for opportunists to play on the emotions of people weakened by the trauma of change and adjustment. Xenophobia, the fear and hatred of foreigners, provided the outlet for the anger and stress of economic instability.

The youth in the East were especially prone to the rhetoric of the right-wing militants coming from the West. Jobs were scarce for adults let alone for the younger generation. The collapse of traditional youth groups that were supported by the Communist Party resulted in the closing of clubs and meeting places where the young people met and socialized. Increased demands in school, including the changes in curriculum to insure integration with the West, forced students to adjust quickly. If a young person failed in school, the most probable result was unemployment, with no apparent relief in the immediate future. Bored teenagers with no prospects for work and unable to pursue studies became targets for western neo-Nazis who filtered into the East, bringing with them a sense of organization and a clear-cut argument justifying the failures in the east, placing the blame on foreigners.

It quickly became evident that most easterners were interested in jobs and their quality of life. Watching their new brethren in the West, it became quite clear that there was a definitive division between the wealthy West Germans who long ago had become affluent and used to a quality of life that was one of the highest in the world and those who had been under Communist rule since World War II. This disparity became obvious as easterners traveled west, many for the first time.

"Ossies" versus "Wessies," or easterners versus westerners, became common journalistic terminology when referring to the growing disparity of East and West Germany. Articles proliferated in the newspapers and magazines expounding on the stark differences between the two divergent peoples and economies. The basis of this dichotomy was the affluent West versus an economically crippled East.

A cornerstone of this issue was the movement on the part of the government of the newly unified Germany to solve the private property dilemma. After unification, many in the West still felt that they had family property claims in the eastern states. Under Communism, these properties were appropriated by the East German government and then given to those who were living in the postwar East Germany. Unification opened the opportunity for displaced families who had lost these lands to file once again for rightful ownership. Westerners came into the communities with a desire to assume those rights, causing friction and spreading a sense of fear among those who had lived there for, in many cases, over forty-five years. Although the residents had never enjoyed a full ownership rights relationship with property, they did feel anger and despair at the thought of having to leave familiar surroundings or to pay a rent that was, in their minds, unfairly placed on their "homes."

By late 1991, the concept of unification became tarnished in both East and West Germany. Capitalism no longer appeared to be the answer to all East German problems. East German society was used to the benefits associated with a Socialist state. Child care, women's employment opportunities, and health care were important assets of a now-defunct system. The easterners did not want to compromise on these needs, making western capitalism less desirable without the addition of the social benefits. The facts that each family must pay for child care, that women were the first to lose jobs in a new market economy, and that health care was predicated on western German programs played key roles in causing consternation and a feeling of inferiority among the East German population. Westerners became less supportive of the financial burdens associated with bringing the two regions together. The glory of October 3, 1990, waned in many minds, and the hard reality of truly unifying two cultures with only language left as a common denominator set the stage for at least the next decade.

Markus Megel, the former foreign minister for the German Democratic Republic and elected to the German Bundestag in 1993 as a Social Democratic (SPD) deputy, provided the sobering possibility of increased right-wing activity in the eastern regions of Germany during his speech of August 13, 1993. He had little good to say about unification and was blunt about the possible unanticipated hazards associated with being like the West.

For over forty-five years the East Germans had known nothing other than a dictatorship that was predicated on Socialist values and under the watchful eye of Moscow. As a member of the eastern bloc, East Germany (GDR) became a model of the most reliable surrogate Communist state. The economy was intertwined with that of the Soviet Union, insuring almost total dependency for the German nation. Large numbers of Soviet military forces occupied the region because it was the potential springboard against western forces. East Germany was an essential partner in the Warsaw Pact. Socialism became deeply entrenched in East German society. Women expected to work alongside men. Children were cared for by state-run programs. Health care, although somewhat primitive, was expected to be made available at subsidized prices, even though waiting in long lines was the norm. Life was generally dull with very few luxuries, but a sense of complacency was instilled in the population because basic needs were met. The glitter of the West seen on television sets in the East provided a sense of longing for the lifestyle enjoyed by their brethren in the Federal Republic of Germany. Although this desire was common, the fear of change and the fear of losing the basic government-sponsored benefits dampened the desire to embrace wholeheartedly western capitalism. The neo-Nazis provided some compromise by supporting the basic need of the "freed" East Germans and blaming the overindulgence of the western states on the other western nations. They argued that a dictatorship by Germans for Germans was the best way for a unified Germany to evolve.

Many citizens in the East still believed that authoritative government was the best option. As the populace developed a growing dislike of the capitalist ways and the tendency to blame politicians, it provided fertile opportunities for those who offered seemingly positive alternatives. The friction between eastern and western populations began to color the attitudes between these apparently different cultures. Easterners saw the westerners as interlopers who were trying to force capitalism and societal changes on a region that was unable or unwilling to change rapidly. The westerners, on the other hand, saw the East as a financial drain that resulted in increased taxes and a source of poor-quality labor that seemed to have no interest in working for maximum profit. Germans in the West tended to focus on the issues that directly affected the western states, giving the impression that the problems in the East were not important. The youth saw little to look forward to as they lounged around home or at the local bars with nothing to do, little chance of employment, and a growing frustration with having no control over their lives.

Old-line Communist Party members also had to adjust to the changing scene. No longer were they the dominant force in local politics, therefore they were forced to adjust their priorities to best take advantage of the changing environment. Many became devout supporters of right-wing rhetoric, moving toward a political system that would best support their experiences as trained authoritarian leaders and administrators. This formed a small but effective passive and active support system for both right-wing extremist political parties and militant organizations.

Playing on the emotions and fears of the East Germans, the neo-Nazis were capable of rapidly moving into the new states and organizing new cells. The youths' frustrations insured a fertile area for developing aggressive organizations that were prone to violence. Punks, hippies, neo-Nazis, and skinheads in the GDR all had their own ways of rebelling. They were all, however, aligned against the Communist state. Following the disintegration of the GDR, these groups channeled their energies into street fighting using the newfound freedoms associated with the move to democracy. Unemployment insured that membership was readily available to support neo-Nazi activities and that the favorite right-wing targets, foreigners, provided the incentive to attract members. Finally, the militants used unification as a reason for attracting supporters. Long advocates of a "greater Germany," the right-wing extremists and militants found new advocates simply because the rightists espoused unification so vehemently for many years. A unified Germany provided the opportunity to realize right-wing dreams of a nation that was once again a major power in Central Europe, common in language and tradition and capable of dictating the political and economic future of the continental nations.

The growing sense of frustration in East Germany became critical in early 1992. The Germans' perception that asylum seekers, who were entering unified Germany in unprecedented numbers, were overwhelming the nation's ability to meet the needs of the common citizens sent a shock wave throughout Germany. East Germans felt themselves to be economically inferior and politically disadvantaged by the West, leading to a common definition of German nationalism by utilizing a new patriotism supported by the right-wing militants. Increased violence from neo-Nazis during this period generally was tolerated by the eastern populace and in many cases applauded by the general masses. It was not until the end of 1992 that support of right-wing violence began to wane as neo-Nazi activities became more violent and threatening.

What attracted the young people to the neo-Nazi movement following unification? Was there an ideological basis that influenced the average recruit? Or was this a fad that provided a means of escape from the pain of change? Research suggests that the average member of these neo-Nazi groups is not oriented to an ideological approach to involvement. They are recruited often by the offering of a common bond with others of similar economic disadvantage. Ideology appears to have been primarily the interest of the leaders and their immediate lieutenants. Even the leaders' approach to a common neo-Nazi doctrine was often not well defined. The neo-Nazis tended to have a rather loose interpretation of what they believed and what they supported. They claimed no clear theoretical and dogmatic basis, but suggested some basic principles. Until the early 1980s, the majority of the neo-Nazi groups appeared to support a semblance of the old Nazi ideology. This was probably the direct result of the influence of the waning Nazi generation, which subtly insured that the years of the Third Reich were not totally forgotten by any who would listen. As the younger leadership became more involved, a change in ideological concepts occurred. Several neo-Nazis began to question Hitler's support and cooperation with the German industrialists. This, they claimed, was a betrayal of true National Socialism. In looking for a more palatable basis for the new neo-Nazi ideology, many of these new members chose to follow figures from the early ideological phase of National Socialism. They began to identify with the NSDAP of the 1920s, particularly the arguments of Otto and Gregor Strasser. In addition, they turned against multi-cultural peoples and supported anti-imperialism, vocalized sympathy for the Palestinians, and argued against capitalism as a state doctrine.

Drawing on the early NSDAP principles incorporated in the twenty-five points drawn up by Hitler, Anton Drexler, and Gottfried Feder in February 1920, the new right-wing incorporated the ideals of nationalism, anti-Semitism, and a distrust of capitalism, big business, and large landowners to mold their limited ideology of the 1990s. Realizing that using the model of Hitler's Third Reich was not beneficial for their future, these same leaders of the neo-Nazi movement began the re-evaluation of the historical aspects of the NSDAP, looking for the root ideology that best symbolized the issues of modern Germany. They found the answers in a mixture of concepts, heavily supported by the Strasser brothers' ideals. Otto and Gregor Strasser's Socialist approach to Nazism rapidly supplanted the old traditional Nazi ideology during the neo-Nazi growth period of the early 1990s. Many neo-Nazis claimed that the Strasser brothers provided a pure approach that was not tainted by compromise and the events surrounding the war years.

The Strassers were early supporters of the National Socialist Worker's Party. Gregor was an excellent speaker who was highly regarded among the party faithful during the 1920s. He was instrumental in implanting the party in the northern German regions and the Rhineland, areas in which the Nazi Party earlier had been unable to penetrate effectively. A powerfully built man with a strong, charismatic personality, Gregor quickly became a key player in the organization. By 1930 he was considered by many to be the number two man in the party. He was the head of one of the most important offices, that of political organization, and enjoyed the personal trust and liking of many of his political opponents. It has been said by some that he could have replaced Hitler as the effective leader of the NSDAP movement in the post-Putsch period while Hitler languished in prison in Munich. Gregor, however, remained an avid supporter of the party. This did not preclude him from espousing different views, nor from being critical of some of Hitler's decisions. He tended to stress strongly radical views associated with anti-capitalism. This Socialist leaning was almost as virulent as his nationalism. In addition, Gregor criticized Hitler's attitude about centralizing authority in the party and his demand for personal unlimited control.

Gregor Strasser, with the support of his brother Otto, rapidly built an organization in northern Germany that began to rival Hitler's southern Germany structure. The Strasser brothers founded a popular political newspaper, *Berliner Arbeitszeitung* (Berlin Worker's Newspaper), which was edited by Otto and which rapidly increased in its circulation. Gregor introduced a young man to the paper and the NSDAP, Paul Josef Goebbels, who became the editor of a periodical for Nazi Party officials. Goebbels also carried the distinction of being Gregor Strasser's private secretary. The NSDAP in northern Germany was becoming a separate party, based on the strength and character of Gregor Strasser, and supported by such advocates as his brother Otto and the overzealous, ambitious young Josef Goebbels.

Differences between Hitler's concepts of operation and the Strasser's became acute in 1925. On November 22, 1925, the Strassers called a meeting in Hannover of North German district Nazi Party leaders. The meeting was designed to consider issues within the party, particularly those issues concerning property expropriation. The Strassers argued that properties owned by former German royal houses should be confiscated for the state and that the other items of personal property should be considered public domain. Hitler's position, as represented at the meeting by supporters, was that it was not politically beneficial to take such a radical position. He contended that this would alienate a potentially important segment of German society.

The result of the Hannover meeting was a majority support for the Strassers. Gregor and Otto's program was accepted, and a resolution was passed that was designed to clarify the original twenty-five point program developed by Hitler, Drexler, and Feder in 1920 with more specific guidance in dealing with the Socialist portion of the National Socialist Worker's Party platform. The original program called for nationalism, anti-Semitism, and an official position against capitalism, trusts, big industrialists, and landowners of large estates. The Hannover resolution reiterated and strengthened this particular portion of the original twenty-five points. In essence, the new resolution drew an ideological line within the NSDAP between the northern and southern regions and pitted the Strasser brothers against Hitler.

Hitler's response to this apparent revolution within the party was most interesting. Rather than using force and potentially causing a permanent split within the party that would be irreparable, he used his political acumen to outmaneuver the Strassers. Hitler called his own meeting on February 14, 1926, and used his power of persuasion to orchestrate a change of heart of the representatives who had supported the Strassers in Hannover. Of special interest was the move of Josef Goebbels from a Strasser advocate to a supporter of a general move to retain party unity, and hence voting for Hitler's program. Hitler, knowing that Gregor Strasser was still highly thought of in the party, used conciliation to retain this icon of the North German Nazi Party. This enabled Hitler to solidify the power bases of the party throughout Germany. The issue of capitalist versus worker was quietly set aside by Hitler and Gregor Strasser in the spirit of unification. Hitler knew that he needed the power, prestige, and money of Germany's big businesses and the leading capitalists in order to reach the party goals. Gregor Strasser fell into line and became an essential and effective spokesman for the growing NSDAP.

Otto Strasser, on the other hand, continued to plague Hitler. Otto's continued agitation for the worker's position in his paper was a barb that made

Hitler extremely uncomfortable. Comments that blatantly attacked Hitler included the argument that Hitler was, in fact, trying to "strangle the social revolution." Hitler retorted with the comment that "Strasser's Socialism was nothing but Marxism." Otto Strasser continued to publicly decry the fact that the National Socialists were moving away from their founding principles, arguing that industry should be nationalized, and that the industrial leaders should be replaced with a chamber of corporations that would be organized along Fascist lines. Otto's radicalism and bent for socialism in labor caused a rift between himself and his brother Gregor. The brothers' disagreement resulted in a permanent split. Otto was driven from the party while Gregor became a more solid supporter of Hitler's program. Although Otto attempted to develop his own party called the "Black Front," he was unsuccessful and was forced to flee Germany after the 1930 elections.

Gregor Strasser supported Hitler until December 5, 1933. The cracks in their mutual support finally ruptured during 1933, causing Hitler to dismiss Strasser from the party, but this was short-lived. Hitler again re-embraced Strasser in June 1934, considering him to be a good potential ally in the government. It became apparent on June 30, 1934, that the gap between the two men was too deep and that old animosities were not forgotten. On this day, Gregor Strasser was arrested at noon in Berlin, taken to the Prinz Albrechtstrasse prison, and executed as a part of the eradication of the SA and other potential opponents of Hitler during the "Night of the Long Knives."

Adolf Hitler and his cronies overshadowed the early players in the Nationalist Socialist Worker's Party, as the German political forces accepted the Nazis into their midst and the Third Reich was born. Gregor and Otto Strasser became footnotes to history as the viciousness of Hitler's dictatorship supplanted the early ideology of the growing Fascist movement. As with the Strassers, old opponents and potential rivals to Hitler's power were liquidated.

This, however, did not preclude the possibility of later reflection by those who still believed in the basic foundations of Nazism after the failure of Hitler and the NSDAP in 1945. Many of those who still harbored dreams of supporting Nazi concepts long after the war were disposed to try and eliminate those elements deemed as bad and to dwell on the potential that could have been realized using other approaches. Therefore, a revival of the Strasser thesis was one means of re-evaluating Nazism and justifying the possible positive ramifications of a German Fascist program.

Initially, the German right-wing militants, particularly those supporting Karl Heinz Hoffman and Michael Kühnen, used Hitler and the Third Reich as their focal point for their internal propaganda. After unification, there was a stronger movement toward aspects of German fascism that reflected less on Hitler and more on the concepts espoused by the Strasser brothers. This is an interesting ideological adjustment and could very well have been influenced by a number of factors. First, the anti-Hitler sensitivities in both the eastern and western parts of Germany made it difficult for groups to obtain support while using the historically bankrupt ideals of the Third Reich. Additionally, laws that precluded Hitlerite propaganda tended to cause friction between the government and the right-wing militants. Second, the idea that Nazism failed under Hitler's leadership, but that it could have been an effective government for the Germans under different leadership or circumstances, caused a number of the younger neo-Nazis to begin searching for answers. Third, the large number of recruits that were brought into neo-Nazi organizations in the East may very well have had a great influence on the shift in ideological basis. The young generation growing up under Communism, seeing and living the theories of socialism, carried portions of this ideology into the post-Cold War era. Their frustrations associated with unemployment and decreased opportunities provided the situation where capitalism became tainted and the need to find a balance between nationalism and socialism that would justify their movement offered a new approach to the neo-Nazi ideology. The Strasser theory of a pro-worker, anti-capitalist movement that captured the nationalist fervor and provided an authoritative system commensurate with the name National Socialist Worker's Party incorporated the principles that could more easily justify the neo-Nazi movement in a unified Germany.

What is important to note is that there was no definitive neo-Nazi ideology that evolved into a national position. There were many groups that were traditionally classified by the German government as neo-Nazi, yet each developed their own concepts of what and how fascism should be incorporated into modern unified Germany. Most used a semblance of the symbols associated with the Nazi Party, such as the salutes and slogans. They utilized the familiar rhetoric of the old NSDAP that struck fear into the Jews and foreigners during the war years. All of the active neo-Nazi militants were anti-Semitic and anti-foreigner. By supporting the Strassers' philosophy of National Socialism, many were attempting to justify their existence as being a separate entity from the historical baggage carried by Hitler's party. Therefore, they reasoned that they should be legally able to pursue their quest of political or societal acceptance. This, however, did not supplant the fact that the neo-Nazis were a dangerous influence in a democracy. Their apparent disregard for democratic principles, their open bias against foreigners and Jews, their rebellion against society, and the growing effort to unify rightist militants throughout Europe were sobering and frightening aspects of a movement born out of a period of German history that is considered to be the most devastating and ill-conceived in the twentieth century.

NOTES

1. Ingo Hasselbach, "How Nazis Are Made," *The New Yorker* (January 8, 1996), 42.

2. Ibid., 43.

3. Ibid., 48.

4. Michael Kühnen died of complications from Acquired Immunodeficiency Syndrome (AIDS) on April 25, 1991. There were reports that Kühnen was a homosexual and that he carried the virus for a number of years before his death, with reports as early as 1988. One of his most ardent followers, Ingo Hasselbach, leader of the East Berlin neo-Nazi group, National Alternative (NA), verified Kühnen's disease in his article "How Nazis Are Made." Hasselbach went on to say that Kühnen's homosexuality eventually split the neo-Nazi movement into "Kühnen loyals" and "anti-gays." The dispute within the movement over his homosexuality was never resolved. He responded to those who wrote anti-gay manifestos with his own argument that the brownshirts of the SA were led by the known homosexual, Ernst Roehm, who died in the 1934 purge conducted by the SS. Kühnen went on to suggest that the movement members stop being influenced by "petit-bourgeois morals." Hasselbach indicated in his article that those who truly believed in Kühnen tended to view his homosexuality as an "unfact" that had nothing to do with the leader's ability to guide the neo-Nazi movement. On his last interview in January 1991, he was emaciated and spoke with a hoarse voice. Kühnen purchased a home in Zimmern, Thyringia, and lived out the rest of his life with his girlfriend, Lisa. Interestingly, he did not tell his best friend, Christian Worch, about his disease until March 1991, just a month before his death.

5. Hasselbach, 43.

6. Ibid., 36.

7. Ibid., 41.

8. Ibid.

9. Ibid.

10. Ibid.

11. Ibid., 39.

12. Ibid., 43.

13. Ibid., 46

14. Fred Leuchter was an American who claimed to be an engineer. He traveled to the Auschwitz concentration camp to determine through scientific means whether the Nazis had gassed people with Zyklon B. Using what he said was the "best scientific equipment," Leuchter presumably measured chemical residue in areas of the camp where there were supposedly gas chambers. The result of these "scientific" studies

was his claim that he conclusively proved that people could not have been gassed with Zyklon B at Auschwitz. He wrote an article entitled "The Auschwitz Lie," which became an important piece of literature among Nazis and neo-Nazis throughout the 1980s and 1990s.

During Ingo Hasselbach's period of re-evaluation of neo-Nazi ideology, he and his brother re-investigated the Leuchter thesis. They found that the report was written in a "ridiculous" style and that the evidence was only superficially scientific. In addition, Ingo, upon further research, noticed that Leuchter had taken his samples from areas that had been completely rebuilt prior to his study. Other areas had flooded regularly over the years, which most likely would have disbursed the cyanide into the groundwater in the intervening forty years. Ingo finally surmised that "the entire basis of the forensic examination was ludicrous."

15. Hasselbach, 47.
16. Ibid., 51.
17. Ibid., 36.
18. Ibid.
19. Ibid.
20. Ibid., 51.
21. Ibid., 47.

4

The New Soldiers

My greatest concern is that this potential for violence [skinhead] could fall into the hands of neo-Nazi groups and that they might use the skins as their militant or military arm.

—Eckhart Werthebach, Radio Interview, *This Week in Germany*, November 25, 1992

Unification of East and West Germany into the new Federal Republic of Germany brought with it a Fascist revival that was largely unexpected. Those in the West who had followed the fortunes of the neo-Nazis in western Germany had little idea of what to expect in the East. The fall of the Berlin Wall and the opening of East Germany to democracy provided a new insight into the right-wing potential that was simmering in the old Democratic German Republic (GDR). An explosion of membership seemed to occur during the first year following unification. Incidents of violence and harassment began to occur far more frequently with larger numbers of participants and a wider selection of targets. The aggressiveness of these new militants was most likely a response to the growing frustrations associated with unification and the dichotomy of wanting both worlds, socialism and capitalism.

Right-wing political parties officially distanced themselves from the neo-Nazi groups prior to the unification. This left many militant organizations without the political clout they hoped would come as a result of providing support to right-wing candidates. The inability of these neo-Nazi organizations to become attached to the credible political scene forced many to once again revert to underground activities that were outside the law. Terrorism became the primary weapon for the post-Cold War neo-Nazi and associated skinheads.

Extremist political parties such as the *Nationaldemocratische Partei Deutschland* (NPD), the *Republikaner Partei* (REP), and the German People's Union (GPU), although officially distancing themselves from these militant groups, continued to retain contacts unofficially throughout the militant community. They did this by using the militant right-wing membership as support elements in a cooperative effort to elect right-wing extremist candidates, particularly in local elections. In most cases, these militants were used to disseminate election materials and to provide vocal support at party rallies.

Although there were continued underground relations between political parties and militants, there were many right-wing extremists within the newly unified Germany and in Austria who found political opportunities too cumbersome to pursue. These were the most militant of the neo-Nazis, often the young, unemployed men with plenty of time to waste and frustrations to vent. Their opportunities were tied to small neo-Nazi groups whose leaders used virulent anti-foreigner rhetoric to capture the imaginations and energies of this disaffected section of German society.

Skinheads, a phenomenon of the 1970s and 1980s, became the "brownshirts" of the neo-Nazi movement. Generally considered to be youthful ruffians with little ideological basis, these young people vented their energies against the establishment and foreigners by using force and harassment.

Three distinct types of skinheads evolved in 1990. Each group wore distinguishing items or colors, similar to the gangs in the United States. The left-wing groups were called "Redskins"; they wore red shoelaces in their boots as an identifier. The right-wing militant groups were referred to as the "Whiteskins"; they wore distinctive white laces in their boots, which designated the wearers as supporters of white power. A third group of "skins" called themselves "SHARP-skins," or Skinheads Against Racial Prejudice. Of these three classes, the Reds and Whites were the militants, often fighting between themselves or against society.

The skinhead movement began in England during the 1970s, and quickly moved across the channel into Europe and across the Atlantic to the United States. Fairly well entrenched in West Germany by the time of unification, these teenagers and young adults, often sporting swastika tatoos, tight jeans, suspenders, boots, t-shirts, leather bomber jackets, and shaved heads, used brutality to express their feelings and gain attention. Music and soccer games provided the social gathering for this gang-type social order. Oi, a type of hard-rock music that utilized lyrics to express distrust of society and the need to use brutal means to gain attention, became big business. This media means, controlled for the most part by Herbert Egoldt under the label "Rock-O-Rama," linked skins and neo-Nazis with millions of latchkey children looking for something to do, someone to blame, or some way to pass the time. Government officials banned numerous songs and music groups that were associated directly with Oi, using the argument that many of the songs included illegal Nazi language. This music was officially classified as *Volksverbetzung*, which meant that it was used to incite young people through the use of negative propaganda. In most cases, the larger stores in Germany that carried music did not stock Oi because of the issue of legality. Most youngsters easily obtained the tapes and CDs at the little shops throughout the country where government officials and police seldom checked.

Traditionally, Oi concerts were the traditional principle vehicle to gather the skinhead population and to hold a semblance of a meeting. An example was the March 14, 1992, concert held near Weimar, Germany, where approximately 1,000 participants gathered to listen to featured German groups such as *Radikahl, Störkraft , Maertyrer, Kraftschlag,* and *Wotan.* All of these groups were well-known right-wing extremist bands who readily supplied music for rightist concerts, aiding the spread of information and dissention within the skinhead scene. Most of the music was heavy-metal rock that expounded the pleasures of genocide.

The popular music group *Störkraft* (Disturbing Force) was considered to be one of the leading bands in the right-wing extremist scene. The group's lead singer and composer, Jörg Petritsch, a twenty-four year old musician, was tried and fined for incitement for using pro-Nazi propaganda and symbols in his lyrics and on the stage.

Another means of reaching the younger generation with this warped propaganda was through the printed media. Comic books, similar to the "superhero" comics available in the United States for young people, provided sinister material that supported Fascist interests. These booklets became widespread in the early 1990s. They were available for anyone who enjoyed the simplicity of pictures and short themes. Invariably, these magazines suggested that killing opponents of right-wing principles was an accepted practice for the betterment of German society. Other magazines, called "fanzines," such as *Der Aktivist, Sachsens Glanz,* and *Volkstreue*, were published sporadically but were designed to exploit the weaknesses of bored and frustrated youth throughout unified Germany.

The skinhead movement quickly moved into the eastern states following unification. Western German influences clearly were apparent in the rapidity of the growth of the eastern skinhead population, as individuals from existing organizations opened up new chapters throughout East Germany. Membership expanded quickly as the children and youth in the new *Länder* searched for an identity. These young people were frustrated by not understanding why, after obtaining their freedom from Communism on November 9, 1989, they still were without jobs and opportunities. This left them with a deep sense of disappointment.

The media and government officials often referred to neo-Nazis and skinheads as being the same. This was a misnomer. Ideologically, the average skinhead was fairly primitive. Many used the phrase "Heil Hitler," but very few knew much about Hitler or World War II. The one thing that they seemed to know was that Hitler eliminated people that were "different." The neo-Nazi leadership used some of these fairly unsophisticated ruffians as a paramilitary force, reminiscent of Hitler's SA "brownshirts."

Although not particularly politically astute, the skinheads enjoyed some recognition from low-level functionaries in the different radical right-wing parties. Representatives from the Republikaner and German People's Union often "hung out" at skinhead clubs, organized and participated in marches, and offered odd jobs to individual skinheads.[1] The respective parties, of course, did not officially sanction these contacts.

The militant neo-Nazis, however, did overtly use many of these young extremists as a semi-paramilitary force in support of political functions and activities that required the use of bullies. In some cases, individual skinheads found an ideological home with the more militant and radical neo-Nazi organizations. Eckhart Werthebach, president of the Office for the Protection of the Constitution, *Verfassungsschutz*, commented during a radio interview on November 25, 1992, that "my greatest concern is that this potential for violence [skinheads] could fall into the hands of neo-Nazi groups and that they might use the skins as their militant or military arm." Interestingly, this had happened on a small scale long before he made these comments. There is little doubt that skinheads supported neo-Nazi groups throughout West Germany prior to unification, and that these groups of young hoodlums participated in post-unification activities. Widespread skinhead support was not apparent, and it appeared to be too difficult to mobilize this portion of right-wing extremist society into a fully operational paramilitary. This was due to the lack of ideological commitment that seemed to permeate the skinhead movement.

There have been a number of theories of why young people became involved in the skinhead movement. Psychologists suggested that this phenomenon was a result of an "inter-generational conflict." The young people had difficulty identifying with the present and therefore fell back on their grandfathers and the

Third Reich. This may have been the result of the efforts to hide the historical past of the Germans in schools, where the twelve years of Hitler's leadership literally were expunged from most of the curriculums.

The economists argued that the skinheads were a result of an underclass with little or no access to society or jobs. These specialists tended to place the blame directly on the economic foundation of modern Germany. The fact that a good number of the skinhead participants were apprentices with technical school training and often employed in factories did not seem to overcome the economists arguments.

Sociologists theorized that the skinheads were something "new." They suggested that the young people involved were "children of industrialization" who were unable to meet the demands of a rapidly changing technologically oriented world. These academics suggested that the skinheads "represented the isolation of an individual in the industrial world."[2]

At the grass-roots level, the social workers saw these young people as being susceptible to skinhead violence because they came from dysfunctional families. They were raised in a violent, abusive, and collapsed family environment where there was "no positive experience and no positive relationship."[3]

Although all of these theories seem to fit characteristics of the skinhead population in general, no single answer appears to explain the growth nor the violence associated with the movement during the late 1980s and immediate post-unification period. Members of the most violent and active groups throughout Germany showed a cross-section of young people from varying backgrounds and different upbringings. It is as if they were missing something in their lives in common. The issue of identity crisis carries a great amount of credence when one considers the variations associated with such a radical movement. This may be a direct result of the Allies' efforts following the war to stamp out Nazism by attempting to exorcise everything to do with the Third Reich, thereby leaving a void in the lives of modern Germans who did not remember the war and had little understanding of those times.

Of the estimated 4,200 active skinheads in Germany, it was difficult to ascertain the total numbers who supported neo-Nazi organizations. It is known that many of these neo-Nazi groups had several hundred skinheads that appeared to be used as a semblance of a military arm. Officials in the city of Hamburg, Germany, estimated that approximately one-quarter of the 300 skinheads identified in that city were also neo-Nazi supporters. This figure seemed to have been arrived at by counting the number of incidents that resulted in judicial charges brought against skinheads in 1993.

With increased police pressure on skinheads throughout Germany, an increasingly larger number began to change their image during the latter part of

1993. Rather than the traditional vestiges of the skin movement, these "new skinheads" began to dress as normal German citizens. Gone were the cropped hairdos, the jeans, boots, and leather jackets. They then sported clothing that made it difficult to identify them as skinheads and thereby increased opportunities to rent apartments and get jobs. This change did not change their attitudes about society, but it allowed them flexibility within the existing social order.

The brutality associated with the modern skinhead of post-unification Germany became well known during the early 1990s. Incidents where both foreigners and Germans alike were attacked, maimed, or killed became commonplace during this time. In 1992, right-wing "Whiteskins" killed seventeen people in Germany. Nine more were killed in the first six months of 1993. Government officials held the skins responsible for over 3,000 attacks during the early months of 1993, with an average of five per day in the early summer. Approximately forty percent of these incidents took place in the new eastern *Länder*.

Two skinheads admitted killing a fifty-three year old unemployed salesman in November 1992. The victim, Karl Heinz Rohm, was Jewish. The two perpetrators, aged eighteen and twenty-four, beat the man almost to death, and then borrowed the bartender's car to haul the dying victim over the German border to the Dutch town of Venlo, where they dumped him and let him die.

At the end of April 1993, eighty "Whiteskins" met in Cottbus, Germany, near the Polish border for an organized gathering. Five nights later there were attacks all across Germany: four against foreigners, three desecrations of Jewish cemeteries, and one attack on a Turkish restaurant. In another act of violence during 1993, skinheads attacked a man and killed him because he "looked Jewish," although the victim could very well have been Christian.

Skinhead violence was not sophisticated. The perpetrators normally did not use a clear-cut plan of attack and seldom identified the victims prior to the attack. Often it was spur-of-the-moment or precipitated by emotion and rumor. The acts clearly were performed in a crude manner with little regard for the law or the potential consequences. The brutality of these acts and the overt disregard for individual rights and property placed the militant skinhead into the criminal fringe. The more sophisticated right-wing militant groups then could call upon these "soldiers" to handle the delicate activities of intimidation and destruction without endangering the primary employer. The skinhead was expendable.

Neo-Nazi groups throughout Germany used these skinheads as needed. Within the neo-Nazi organizations themselves there were numerous members who had no hesitation in pursuing the most aggressive tactics to obtain their goals. Michael Kühnen's group survived a number of government attempts to ban and disrupt their activities. The result was a fairly resilient neo-Nazi organization that quickly adopted. Kühnen was able to develop a core organization that continued to thrive despite the numerous government bans and police raids. Kühnen's death from AIDS in the Spring of 1991 did not spell the end to this virulent neo-Nazi group. From late 1989 to 1991, Kühnen worked extremely hard to cement a common neo-Nazi movement in Europe. He left a legacy for the eventual joining together of a number of groups throughout Germany that solidified the militant right-wing in the unified Federal Republic and insured an international flavor with coordination between German, Austrian, Dutch, Belgian, and French neo-Nazis.

Although many of the neo-Nazi groups retained a semblance of independence, there were some leaders who quickly moved to the forefront to replace Michael Kühnen as the primary spokesman for the Central European militants. Initially, Kühnen was replaced by a young Austrian neo-Nazi, Gottfried Küssel, an even more militant follower of the Nazi traditions and a member of the international neo-Nazi group, the National Socialist Worker's Party-Overseas Organization (NSDAP-OA). Küssel claimed to have been named as Kühnen's successor by the infamous leader on his deathbed. He had an unshakable and fervent belief in a Fourth Reich. What was important was that Küssel did not have the patience of Kühnen and was in a hurry to assume full control of both the Austrian and German governments. His first priority was setting up concentration camps that would quickly solve the "problem" of Jews and subversives before they could undermine the new regime.[4] He also placed great emphasis on the theory that National Socialism should be an overall biological program, which included the environment. His followers often spent time cleaning up certain areas and "hiking alongside tourists like Boy Scouts."[5]

Küssel immediately developed closer ties with neo-Nazi contacts within Germany and the United States. Building on a pre-unification relationship, he began dealing with Gary Rex Lauck, a virulent activist in Lincoln, Nebraska, and the accepted leader of the propaganda organization referred to as NSDAP-OA. Lauck provided vast amounts of printed neo-Nazi literature to Europe during the previous ten years and was intimately involved in international neo-Nazi activities.

Küssel became more vocal and more dangerous throughout the latter part of 1991 and early 1992. He developed programs to provide terrorist and guerrilla training for his supporters. He openly flaunted his neo-Nazism and verbally espoused his desire to use force to overthrow the German governmental system, eliminate foreigners and Jews, and to set up a new Nazi stronghold in Central Europe. His apartment in the upperclass Bezirk area of Vienna was a shrine to the Nazis. At the front door entrance were wax figures of SS soldiers in full uniform. In the bathroom, the toilet bowl had a yellow enamel Star of David painted inside, so that Küssel's followers could urinate on the "hated symbol."[6] His dining room was like a general's headquarters. In the center was a long polished oak table surrounded by high-backed chairs. A full swastika flag hung from a pole in the corner.[7]

Küssel's ego and sense of power led him to an interview with a filmmaker from Sweden, which then was aired in March 1992 over network television in the United States as a part of an investigative story dealing with the rise of right-wing extremism in Germany. In addition, he provided *Prime-Time Live* with a tour of a paramilitary camp. As if this was not enough, Küssel was interviewed by *Nightline*, where he praised Hitler, called the gas chambers of the Third Reich a hoax, and taunted Beate Klarsfeld, who had dedicated her life to bringing Nazis to justice.

Gottfried Küssel, the thirty-five year old extremist, was arrested on January 7, 1992, and convicted in an Austrian court of violating laws dealing with attempting to renew National Socialist activity. He could have been sentenced to life in prison, but was only sentenced to ten years. Although Küssel was imprisoned for his activism, the fact remained that right-wing militarism was not dead; it was planted not only in the fertile German society that was groping for identity, equality, and opportunity in an era of extreme difficulty brought on by the frustrations associated with unification, but also in neighboring regions. Küssel was succeeded in Austria by Gerhard Endres in Vienna and Jürgen Lipthay in Salzburg.

Gottfried Küssel was only one example of the growing strength of post-Kühnen leadership. Christian Worch, an early supporter and effective lieutenant of Kühnen, became the nominal leader in central and northern Germany. Worch, a thirty-seven year old Hamburg resident, already had a reputation as the leader of the notorious *Nationale Liste* neo-Nazi group. This was an organization that was made up of Kühnen supporters who were also in the *Freiheitliche Deutsche Arbeiterpartei*, a political neo-Nazi group centered in the Hamburg area that was organized in 1989 as a party of the new Nationalists.

Christian Worch was quite different than his protege, Michael Kühnen. He was known to have inherited a great deal of money, making him one of the richest neo-Nazi members. Worch had a history of contributing lavish gifts and supplies to the movement, making him a valuable resource, but this did not defray the fact that his cold personality tended to keep him aloof from most of the members.

An excellent organizer and effective promoter, Worch continued Kühnen's efforts to solidify the neo-Nazi movement in Germany and northern Europe. He was the primary organizer and promoter for the August 14, 1993, march in Fulda, Germany, in remembrance of Rudolf Hess. Earlier, in 1990, he was active in supporting the development of the National Alternative right-wing militant movement in East Berlin, which enhanced Kühnen's efforts to move east. Worch personally made a great number of valuable contacts in the East that resulted in a number of arranged visits and jointly sponsored demonstrations. These efforts solidified Worch as a known quantity in the neo-Nazi movement, providing impetus for his elevation as a leader following Kühnen's death in 1991.

Working with Thomas Wulff, aged thirty, Worch consolidated the position of *Nationale Liste* (NL) in the neo-Nazi community. This particular group assumed a political platform for their "Party of New Nationalism," which was included in a catalog for the Hamburg city elections to be held on September 12, 1993. This platform was based on four major issues. First, they supported "children's playgrounds for German children." Second, they argued that all foreigners who were criminals or unemployed should be sent out of the Hamburg area. Third, they insisted that asylum to Hamburg be immediately stopped. And fourth, they wanted asylum gangs in Hamburg neighborhoods to be broken up. This platform against foreigners became the source of political turbulence in Hamburg just prior to the elections. The result was that the Hamburg senate banned the *Nationale Liste* as an organization in August 1993, eliminating them from participating as a political entity.

This proved to be only a small setback for Worch and Wulff. Worch, in particular, continued to develop an international neo-Nazi movement begun by Kühnen before his death from AIDS on April 25, 1991. This movement was called *Gessinnungsgemeinschaft der Neuen Front* (Community of Partisans of the New Front) and was specifically designed to bring the many divergent right-wing militant groups together in a common front working together to meet their similar goals. This organization's primary objective was to obtain the repeal of the ban on Nazis and the rebuilding of the NSDAP as a legal party. The movement brought together such diverse leaders as Worch, Roeder, and Künter Reinholder from Germany, Thomas Bhino from Denmark, Küssel from Austria, and Lauck from the United States. In essence, the neo-Nazi movement moved into a new era following unification. There was new leadership with an international flair that showed a willingness to use open force and realized the importance of consolidating resources.

The militant right-wing became even more effective and aggressive during the immediate post-unification years. German unification brought together two nations, each with its rightist baggage. In 1992, a new and fearful strength became evident among the neo-Nazis. Using young people who were bored, unemployed, and susceptible to radicalism, rightist militants forged an unruly army of adherents who were pulled together under the common theme of anti-asylum for foreigners in Germany. The right-wing extremist leadership, using the argument that foreigners were diluting German society and taking valuable jobs, obtained a following that was far more aggressive and visible than at any time during the Cold War period. In Berlin, Hasselbach's National Alternative organization moved to terrorism as a means of expressing their dislike for the government. They wanted to strike targets that would seriously damage democracy throughout Germany. Targets initially considered included Gregor Gysi, head of the Party for Democratic Socialism, which was the successor to the defunct Communist Party. Others who were discussed as possible assassination targets included Ignatz Bubis, head of the Jewish community in Germany, Chancellor Kohl, and the Domestic Affairs Minister, along with a number of politicians in Bonn.[8]

Although these ideas never came to fruition, primarily because of Hasselbach's defection from the neo-Nazis, they were indications of the potential effort associated with the right-wing militants in 1992. Interestingly, neo-Nazi groups such as the NA found plenty of sources that helped prepare them for the move into terrorism. One of the most useful manuals obtained was published by the U.S. Army. This publication, called "Explosives and Demolitions," was photocopied and sent to neo-Nazis all over Germany.[9] The most modern handbook dealing with terrorism was sent from Gary Lauck's NSDAP-OA in Nebraska via the electronic Internet system. This computer handbook was called "A Movement In Arms," and it described how to wage terrorist war against a democratic government.[10] This move towards neo-Nazi terrorism caused the German government a great deal of concern and anxiety during an important era of change and adjustment.

The German government provided the seed for the neo-Nazi anti-foreigner rhetoric. In order to rebuild a devastated war-torn nation following World War II, German government policies supported the immigration of guest workers into West Germany to do the more menial tasks that many Germans were not interested in doing. This was considered by the post-war government in the 1960s to have been essential for the rapid and effective construction of the German economy. The efforts to obtain an additional work force to meet the growing demands of a growing economic power were a boon to Germany. The immigrant workers filled an important void in the German work force, supplying labor in the unskilled markets when it was difficult to obtain sufficient support from the indigenous population. During the 1960s and 1970s, this injection of new labor was extremely important to the growth of the German economy. Unification, however, obscured the obvious benefits derived from the "guest worker" concept. With unification came the high costs associated with bringing two divergent economies together, one expanding and robust, the other on the brink of complete failure. Unemployment tended to focus the problems in the economy on the immigrants. The right-wing seized on this issue as the primary reason for the dilution of German society and the apparent lack of employment opportunities for Germans, particularly the younger generation.

The right-wing arguments bitterly pointed out that foreigners brought into Germany under the guise of the "guest worker" program and the influx of asylum seekers leaving their homelands and coming to Germany were the cause of Germany's economic problems. The rightists readily skewed this view to their benefit. German laws, particularly the Basic Law, which was originally intended only as a temporary framework for a future constitution, supported open immigration for the asylum of oppressed peoples since its adoption in 1949. The numbers of these immigrants far outnumbered those who were permitted to enter Germany as guest workers. During 1992, government officials estimated that 400,000 to 500,000 refugees from as many as forty countries entered Germany. This was double the number who immigrated to Germany during the previous year. Most of these people intended to apply for residency in Germany under the liberal policies dealing with asylum.[11] Out of this large number, less than five percent ultimately would be allowed to remain. The legal system proved to be slow in determining the eligibility of these immigrants, often taking years rather than months to make a final decision. The large number of asylum seekers then were placed into the German economy until their cases could be heard. During this time, the different states were required to house and feed these people. There were many refugees who were, in many cases, forbidden by law to work once they arrived in Germany. German farmers also imported over 200,000 immigrant workers per year to make up for labor shortages.[12] This, in addition to the large number of asylum seekers, gave some credence to the right-wing arguments against continued immigration policies. This seemed to many to place an additional burden on the local economies and the federal social system, hence providing the appearance that Germany was being inundated by foreigners. Actually, the costs to Germany were only a fraction of what it cost to support over 3.5 million unemployed Germans during the immediate post-unification years. Therefore, the right-wing extremists used perception, rather than fact, as the basis to develop a following using the immigration policy as the basic political weapon.

Another major issue that the neo-Nazis capitalized on was the apparent disregard that many of the foreigners showed for Germanic traditions and culture. A good number of the guest workers and asylum seekers who were granted the privilege of remaining in Germany favored retaining their own customs and traditions, which were often far different than those of Central Europe. Over the years, the Turks and other nationalities retained their own languages, religious customs, and tended to live in areas that became small colonies of similar immigrants. The children from these families, although growing up in Germany, learned from their elders. This added fuel to the right-wing argument against dilution of Germany and the Germanic culture, as these people looked, talked, and worshipped differently than the majority of German society.

A majority of these legal immigrants, many having lived in Germany for years, never were capable of attaining citizenship. German laws made it extremely difficult for individuals who were not German by blood to become citizens. The overwhelming amount of red tape and the years required to meet minimum requirements excluded almost all of the immigrants. Each applicant had to have worked in Germany for at least fifteen years prior to even starting the process of becoming a full citizen. Out of a total Turkish population of approximately 1.9 million in Germany in 1994, only about 13,000 obtained and carried the legal title of a German citizen. (See Table 4.1.)

TABLE 4.1

Principal German Foreign Populations in 1994

Turkey	1,900,000
Former Yugoslavia	930,000
Italy	563,000
Greece	352,000
Poland	261,000
Austria	186,000

Germany has approximately 6.3 million foreign residents, including foreign workers, their dependents, and students.

Those children who were born in Germany were not given citizenship and faced the eventuality that they would most likely always remain outsiders in German society. The inability to become full-fledged German citizens who enjoyed the full democratic rights associated with citizenship insured that the majority of guest workers and asylum seekers would continue to remain "foreigners" in the eyes of the average German citizen.

Threatened by increased crime, drugs, and the spread of AIDS in the early 1990s, the German people often became willing listeners to right-wing arguments about the "immigration problem." The asylum seekers were the focus of the hate and fear generated by the right-wing agitators throughout

Germany and neighboring countries. They were viewed as freeloaders on the German social system. In the East, many people tolerated, and in some cases applauded, the neo-Nazi violence during 1992. A feeling of "us versus them" [foreigners] prevailed in many areas, particularly those most impacted by unemployment. The neo-Nazis played on the prejudices against *Gastarbeiter* (guest workers), refugees, and immigrants, obtaining support throughout unified Germany from many who normally would not listen to the rantings of the right-wing extremists.

In 1993, the Federal Office for the Protection of the Constitution, *Verfassungsschutz*, a special section of the Ministry of Interior, assumed the responsibility for monitoring the militant right-wing activities. Prior to this time, the criminal justice system was responsible for insuring that illegal activities were adjudicated and controlled. The *Verfassungsschutz* was designed to deal specifically with potential and active groups that posed a threat to the constitutional principles inherent in the Basic Law. This office was the primary government agency that monitored the left-wing activities, such as the Red Army Faction, during the turbulent 1960s and 1970s. However, they were not directly involved in tracking right-wing extremist activities because there appeared to be no real threat to the democratic system. Their annual report, *Verfassungsschutzbericht*, included a section on right-wing extremists beginning in the 1980s. This report section became more voluminous over the ensuing years, and in the three years following unification it became fairly extensive. Officials estimated in 1992 that there were only about 35,000 members of far-right extremist organizations. This appeared to have been a fairly conservative estimate considering that, in the Baden-Württemberg elections of March 1992, over 530,000 people voted for the Republikaner candidates. In addition, thousands participated in numerous marches supporting right-wing extremist rhetoric throughout Germany.

In the eastern states, the right-wing openly organized immediately following unification. Right-wing leadership sought membership throughout the eastern region, particularly targeting the poorer, industrial neighborhoods. Lutz Dronenberger, a twenty-seven year old in Gorbitz, a suburb of Dresden, organized over 300 members into his neo-Nazi group. He offered the young people of the area a new blend of ideology that incorporated old NSDAP programs. Gorbitz was an excellent place to spread neo-Nazism: The unemployment was extremely high, and poverty skyrocketed throughout the entire community. Kronenberger filled the void by offering an emotional socialism that was mixed with romanticism of the past based on the Third Reich.

Wolfgang Brück, a professional sociologist in Leipzig, estimated in early 1992 that at least 50,000 young people in eastern Germany were emotional supporters of right-wing extremism.[13] Bernd Wagner, a German security expert, estimated that there were between 10,000 and 15,000 militant neo-Nazis in the five new states in the east by 1992.[14] These might be conservative estimates considering the large number of activists that marched in eastern cities during 1992. German government officials estimated that approximately 42,000 Germans belonged to neo-Nazi and right-wing extremist groups in 1992 and 1993.[15] It is important to note that the government security agencies said that many of the 3,000 right-wing militant attacks which occurred during those two years were actually only "spontaneous acts of drunken or unruly youths."[16] This suggestion is a good indicator that, as of the summer of 1993, the government was still downplaying the importance of the neo-Nazi and skinheads as organizations.

In 1992, officials identified eighty-two right-wing extremist and neo-Nazi organizations.[17] These groups were credited with obtaining support from twenty-nine publishing companies and marketing firms, seven book publishers, and seventeen newspaper and periodical publishers. Authorities found that approximately seventy-five right-wing publications were being distributed throughout Germany with around fifty-four being published at least quarterly. Circulation exceeded 6.1 million copies in this year alone, and this does not include the large number of publications that were being produced outside of Germany and smuggled into the country. In 1993, the number of publications increased to eighty-six, with a corresponding increase in circulation to 6.5 million copies. The number of book publishers increased to eight, and there were four more newspapers and magazines that catered to right-wing interests. Someone was reading this material, and the producers must have had financial support. It would appear that there was a large underground interest in right-wing extremist views, particularly associated with foreigners, that permeated a large block of German society.

The difficulty in determining the extent of right-wing militancy in Germany is the identification and definition of membership. Often articles and discussions about the extreme right-wing in Germany lump groups together and refer to them all as neo-Nazis. It is imperative that the observer realize that there are variations of right-wing extremism and militancy in Germany which do not necessarily constitute the same level of danger to the democratic system. A more definitive delineation of rightist activity shows a vast difference within the German right-wing movement. For example, the rise of the right-wing political parties in the late 1980s and early 1990s were viewed by many critics as neo-Nazi parties. Traditionally, the National Democratic Party (NPD) had espoused extreme right-wing platforms, but it was a mixture of conservative members that varied in their support of radical concepts. Important was the fact that this party remained on the boundary of legality, and therefore never pushed the government into banning their organization. To call the whole party neo-Nazi was broadening the interpretation of the term to include extremists, radicals, and militants, as well as ultra-conservative law-and-order types of people. This was also true of the other right-wing political parties such as the *Republikaner* and the *Deutsche Volksunion*. This, of course, does not suggest that these extremist right-wing parties have not shown a certain empathy for their more militant and aggressive brothers in the skinhead and neo-Nazi movements. There was ample proof to support the argument that these political organizations used, although surreptitiously, members of these groups to support the more aggressive radical activities of the most extreme elements within the parties.

Even among the so-called neo-Nazi and skinhead groups, there are variations of militancy. Some, such as the *Freiheitliche Deutsche Arbeiterpartei* (FAP), were actively involved in right-wing rhetoric and occasional militant activities, but they walked the fine line of legality. These groups often were involved in political activities that supported their own local candidates or those of the right-wing extremist parties.

The FAP was established in 1979 as a neo-Nazi political organization. In 1986, the leader, Seigfried Müller, was arrested for arson. Government officials began closely observing and tracking FAP activities and members for possible banning. In 1989, this group was the most active neo-Nazi group to participate in the German elections. The more radical members began to split off and organize into far more aggressive and violent splinter groups. These new organizations included the infamous "Sport and Security Comradeship of the Iron Cross First Class," led by Bernd Futter, a thirty year old militant who was implicated in the arson attacks that led to the arrest of Müller. The police used Müller to identify Futter as the perpetrator and leader who was responsible for the arson attacks, resulting in a guilty verdict and prison time for the splinter group leader.

During 1988, Friedhelm Busse, aged sixty-four, assumed control of the FAP. Membership plummeted during the late 1980s as more emphasis was placed on politics and many members left the group to organize more potent neo-Nazi organizations. Dropping from a known membership of approximately 500 in 1987 and 1988 to a low of 220 in 1992, the FAP appeared to be disintegrating. A revival in 1993 showed an increase of approximately 100 percent in membership, resulting in an estimate of 430 active participants. Inherent with this increase was the move back to more aggressive activities. Federal officials became far more cognizant of the rising FAP fortunes in 1993, forcing judicial officers to consider banning the organization totally.

The most militant right-wing extremists, aptly referred to as neo-Nazis, gravitated toward Michael Kühnen's organizations or emulated his program. These were the most potent and dangerous right-wing extremists in Germany. Kühnen's death did not eliminate this threat; instead it actually increased the radicalism under new and dangerous leaders who were unafraid of blatant terrorist warfare against a society they deemed as inadequate for the role that Germany should play in European politics and the need to retain Germanic purity in German society. These were the people who were actively engaged in consolidating the neo-Nazi movement into a European-wide effort to install an authoritarian, law-and-order, anti-foreigner system through the use of violence. The threat these groups posed was real. They utilized the youth of German society to spread their philosophy and to attack the foundations of postwar German democratic ideals. These militants were the true neo-Nazis, using Nazi symbols and spouting slogans reminiscent of the 1920s and 1930s. Many considered them more a nuisance than a threat. They were both.

Neo-Nazis are credited with over thirty deaths of both foreign and German individuals since unification. They wreaked havoc in Jewish cemeteries and in public buildings, and accosted people on public transportation. Their numbers grew following unification, with apparent increases of passive support in many areas of unified Germany as well. Neo-Nazis are not a direct threat to the German governmental system, but they are a threat to individuals living in Germany who are perceived as outsiders or who do not accept the violence that is being wielded by these militant youth.

NOTES

1. "Europe's New Right," *Newsweek* (April 27, 1992), 32.

2. Jane Kramer, "Neo-Nazis: A Chaos In The Head," *The New Yorker* (June 14, 1993), 55.

3. Ibid.

4. Ingo Hasselbach, "How Nazis Are Made," *The New Yorker* (January 8, 1996), 50.

5. Ibid., 45.

6. Ibid., 50.

7. Ibid.

8. Ibid., 51.

9. Ibid., 36.

10. Ibid.

11. Kramer, 55.

12. Torsten Baensch, *Jugendlichen Raum Lassen?* (Hamburg: Lütcke & Wulff, 1992), 43.

13. Kramer, 67.

14. "The Violent Rise of Hitler's New Youth," *World Press Review* (August, 1991), 22.

15. Ibid.

16. *The Stars and Stripes* (September 15, 1993)

17. Bundesminister des Innern, *Verfassungsschutzbericht* (1992).

5

The Explosion

One has to live together. But grow together?
—Thomas Flierl, German Cultural Office, "Still Divided,"
The Stars and Stripes, October 9, 1995

German unification fostered numerous domestic problems, some of which were largely unforeseen. October 3, 1990, marked the beginning of the difficult assimilation of two divergent societies. Right-wing extremism was one of those elements that was not considered a threat to the unifying process. This shortsightedness, however, proved to be an error in planning for a smooth transition. Beginning in early 1991, governmental officials at local levels began to see the viciousness associated with the growing neo-Nazi movement. Long considered a minor but potentially potent menace to West German tranquility, the skinheads and neo-Nazis became a vocal and visual threat to the evolving democratic principles in the eastern *Länder* as unemployment and frustration with the slowness of change set into the population. Attacks on foreigners became widespread throughout the eastern regions of Germany during 1991. The police initially ignored the right-wing extremist and skinhead activities, but they finally were forced to react. Unfortunately, that reaction often was overly severe, forcing the militants to become more aggressive and aligning empathetic supporters with the young neo-Nazis. The inability of the police to develop a strategy that effectively neutralized the evolution of right-wing militancy played a key role in the increasingly blatant violations of the laws designed to eliminate National Socialism and crimes perpetrated by Hitler.

The neo-Nazis and the skinheads showed a new openness that was enacted through violent activities in both eastern and western Germany during the first year after unification. In the city of Schwerin, located in Mecklenburg-Western Pomerania, gangs of young neo-Nazis harassed and threatened Vietnamese street peddlers with bodily harm. Soon afterward, in the city of Dresden in late April of 1991, Jorge Joao Gomondai, a twenty-eight year old Mozambican, was pushed from a moving streetcar by local skinheads and died shortly afterwards from his injuries. His funeral was disrupted by over eighty right-wing youth chanting *"Sieg Heil"* and *"Ausländer Raus"* (foreigners out). In the eastern German city of Görlitz, on the border of Poland, fifteen neo-Nazis attacked a Polish couple, who were sitting in their car, sending them both to the hospital with severe injuries. Then, again in Dresden, skinheads attacked the well-known leftist hangouts of Cafe 100 and the Bronxx Cafe, destroying furniture and setting fire to the structures.

In another act of violence, thirty young German youths forced their way into a Nambibian hostel in the city of Wittenberge and threw two young students out of windows. Early in April of 1991, neo-Nazis rampaged through the streets of Frankfurt on Oder shouting racist slogans and throwing stones at Polish tourists. These are only a sampling of the numerous terrorist acts that occurred in eastern Germany during the first few months following unification. In Dresden alone, over twenty-four acts of violence occurred against foreigners in the first six months after unification. This number included only those incidents in which arrests were made and the perpetrators were adjudicated in the local court system. The local police appeared to be helpless against the onslaught of right-wing militancy and violence. In fact, during the Summer of 1990, police in an East Berlin suburb stood by and watched neo-Nazis led by Küssel attack a hostel for foreign workers. After the attack was completed, the police then moved in and closed off the area.[1]

It is ironic that the youth in the eastern German states became so susceptible to right-wing propaganda. For over forty-five years the people of East Germany were dominated by the authority of Communism. The blind obedience to that authority provided an excellent environment for the present right-wing rhetoric. The dependence on central power supported the argument for nationalism and the need for an authoritative government. This, in conjunction with a xenophobia that became prevalent throughout the eastern region, appeared to evolve during the isolation of East Germany. The fear of outsiders and foreigners was genuine, yet the numbers of foreigners in East Germany, only 191,190 out of a population of 16 million in 1989, indicated an extremely small percentage of outsiders in comparison to West Germany, which had a foreign population of 4.8 million out of 61.5 million. Once again, the lower number of foreigners largely was attributed to the enclosed society that occurred under Soviet control.

It is interesting to note that the most active right-wing extremists in the East were from staunch Communist families. Those who were identified as active militants were often sons of former Communist Party and Secret Police officials. This phenomenon suggested that these young people possibly were searching for opportunity. Not long before, they enjoyed the benefits of Communism, but after the fall of the regime they were looking for their niche in a rapidly changing world where their pasts often became a detriment to advancement. They were cognizant of authority, and they often considered outsiders as people to be feared. Extremism, therefore, provided the means for obtaining the new opportunities and responding to the traditional ingrained beliefs.

The first year following unification was only a harbinger of the future. As 1992 began, the neo-Nazi movement was growing in membership and violence, particularly in the vulnerable East. Over the year, the number of incidents directly attributed to right-wing militants, both neo-Nazi and skinhead, increased by seventy-four percent. There were over 4,000 attacks on foreigners, as these rightist groups targeted immigrants, students, and tourists. Of these 4,000, police officials classified 2,580 as outright acts of violence. A total of fifteen acts of homicide and manslaughter were committed which resulted in seventeen deaths. Neo-Nazis used arson, bombings, and intimidation to salve their mindless aggression. In the one year, fourteen bombings were attributed to these groups. In addition, 708 cases of arson and 725 cases of bodily harm were identified to have been directly related to the growing neo-Nazi and skinhead subcultures. Property damage through the use of graffiti and physical destruction became commonplace with over 1,122 known incidents, particularly against Jewish cemeteries and Turkish residences.

In addition to numerous violent crimes, right-wing militants increased their numbers of propaganda crimes by sixty-five percent during 1992. These illegal activities, over 2,700 cases adjudicated during the year, included those instances where groups disseminated literature or other means of propaganda that used outlawed Nazi materials and references. Moving from the printed forms, neo-Nazi groups began employing computer games and music to spread their illegal propaganda, making it very difficult for authorities to impede or control the use of this type of material.

The neo-Nazi crimes of 1992 were far more vicious than most of those perpetrated prior to unification. Groups of neo-Nazis circulated in public areas looking for victims. A favorite area in Berlin was along the subway routes and at major debarkation points. During November 1992, the citizens of Berlin were shocked by the blatant attacks conducted by these bored young people. Two young men, sixteen and seventeen years old, respectively, stabbed a young man to death on the steps of the subway station in the eastern part of the city. Silvio Meier, a twenty-seven year old transient who was being accompanied by two other men and a woman, was drawn into an altercation with a group of young neo-Nazis, of which the same two youths were involved. The neo-Nazis used knives in the fight, stabbing Meier to death and wounding the other three. When the police interrogated the two young men who were identified as the killers, they readily admitted to having stabbed Meier to death and rationalized their actions by saying that "they had something against foreigners and squatters." The neo-Nazi group considered Meier and his friends to be "squatters," therefore setting the stage for the deadly confrontation.

In another case, officials of a small village with a total population of 260 people directly supported local neo-Nazis in their use of arson to discourage asylum seekers from moving into the town. The village of Dolgenbrot's mayor, Herr Preissler, hired the local right-wing militants to burn down a vacant building that was designated as housing for asylum seekers. Village officials were alleged to have offered the neo-Nazis 2,000 Deutsche Mark, approximately $1,333, and logistical assistance to insure success. This arson attack was the culmination of a number of protests against the housing of sixty asylum seekers in the town. The local citizens felt that the number of immigrants being housed in their village was proportionally too great. With the population only being 260, the people considered the injection of sixty outsiders to be an unacceptable sacrifice for the community.

Once the neo-Nazi ruffians completed their contract and burned down the structure, the locals celebrated in a local tavern. Mayor Preissler, responding to official inquiries, stated that "no one was hurt, therefore nothing had happened." This attitude seemed to permeate the region, fueled by the growing number of asylum seekers who were dependent on German hospitality. Many Germans felt a sense of empathy for the villagers, who they perceived as being subjected to unreasonable governmental requirements. The result was a week-long series of anti-foreigner sieges of asylum facilities throughout the region.

Anti-foreign sentiments pervaded in this area until the Mölln attack in the Fall of 1992. The neo-Nazi murders of a woman and two young girls in the town of Mölln was a primary event in 1992 that galvanized a people's movement opposing violence against foreigners. It also forced the federal government to begin to recognize the real dangers associated with the rising right-wing militant aggressiveness.

In addition to the increasing use of brute violence, after unification the neo-

Nazi groups became far more sophisticated in their means of attracting followers. Traditionally crude in their means of terrorism and propaganda, the newer, more enlightened leaders looked for ways of communicating and indoctrinating potential recruits. In one case, a telephone network was developed between the cities of Wiesbaden, Hallenberg, Sauerland, Mainz, Hamburg, and Ludwigshaven. This network provided a recorded electronic bulletin board for callers who were aware of the correct telephone number.

By the Fall of 1992, a computer mail system was in place. Called THULE, this e-mail program originated in Nürnberg, and allowed text and information to be sent to and between the most infamous right-wing extremist political organizations, the DVU, FAP, and NPD. The concept was to transfer information between these political entities and allow access to international right-wing groups. One of the more important aspects was an information database for all Nationalist activities in Germany.

Neo-Nazi and skinhead activity in Germany during 1992 proved to be the beginning of a three-year spree of violence and crime that had not been seen since the end of the Third Reich. This first year was the worst in postwar German history for right-wing militant violence, resulting in seventeen deaths and over 2,500 acts of brutality linked to the right-wing extremists. No one seemed to be overly worried about this unprecedented increase. It took a tragic incident in the town of Mölln to clarify the problem and force the majority to directly face the issue of a growing neo-Nazi threat. Prior to Mölln, government involvement in controlling right-wing activities was limited to state and local authorities. The public outpouring of rage following the blatant murder of a woman and two children forced the federal government to re-evaluate the role of federal agencies in the restriction of neo-Nazi activities throughout Germany.

Mölln, a small town of approximately 16,000 residents and located in the eastern portion of Schleswig-Holstein, Germany's northern-most state, became internationally famous following the firebomb attack, which resulted in the deaths of children living in one of its residential neighborhoods. Although there had been attacks and threats against foreigners in this area before, it was the arson attack in Mölln in late 1992 that galvanized Chancellor Helmut Kohl's government in Bonn to take initial steps for more aggressive action against the neo-Nazi militant movement throughout Germany.

On the night of November 22, 1992, two young men, Michael Peters and Lars Christiansen, drove up to a residence known to be inhabited by a local Turkish family; with their faces covered by masks, they threw a firebomb into the house and then quickly drove away. The fire spread rapidly, engulfing the residence and the neighboring house within minutes. The owner of the targeted building was a fifty-one year old Turkish woman, Bahide Arslan, who had lived in Germany for years. Bahide, along with her ten year old granddaughter, Yeliz Arslan, and her fourteen year old niece, Ayse Yilma, were in the house when the arsonists struck. The fire sealed off the front entrance of the house, making it difficult for the family to escape. Bahide attempted to rush into the room where the two girls were located, but was unable to bring them to safety. All three died. Before the fire was finally controlled, the two houses were destroyed and nine other residents were injured, some jumping from windows to save themselves.

Michael Peters and Lars Christiansen were arrested within a short time after the attack. A young nine year old girl testified that she saw the two men, wearing masks, drive up in a car like Christiansen's, stop, and throw the infamous firebombs that killed the three people. The public outcry that poured forth from this incident in northern Germany rocked the German government, forcing the leaders of the local and national political parties to take notice of the growing number of violent acts that were becoming more blatant each year since unification. The authorities found that the growing neo-Nazi movement which was feeding on anti-foreigner prejudice, particularly against the Turks, was a direct cause of this attack and was the basis for a series of incidents in every state in Germany.

The police in Mölln were aware that the two perpetrators of this attack were involved in right-wing militant activities. Michael Peters was twenty-five years old at the time of the incident and had never held a steady job. Police officials knew that he was a leader of a gang that was suspected of throwing firebombs at at least two other homes of foreigners in the vicinity of Mölln. Lars Christiansen was a nineteen year old supermarket clerk who used to write anti-foreigner music lyrics and was known to have celebrated Hitler's birthday the previous April with Peters. A search of their apartments resulted in authorities finding Nazi memorabilia and a number of xenophobic posters.

Peters and Christiansen were only two young men out of a large number of militants who were associated with the rising xenophobia in Germany following the unification of Germany on October 3, 1990. They, however, were instrumental in focusing the attention of the public on the need for government involvement in controlling the apparent increase in violent acts that was aimed at not only foreign adults, but which also began to include innocent children. Many of those who read the papers and listened to the news reports of this horrible attack were abhorred at the callousness and open violence that the neo-Nazis were flaunting throughout the Federal Republic of Germany. Chancellor Kohl reacted with a stern statement by referring to the attack in Mölln as being "a disgrace to our country. I can't express it any other way." The *Frankfurt New Press* newspaper was more blunt in an editorial claiming that, "for at least two years [since unification] we've been awash in a wave of violent right-wing extremist acts against foreigners; the appalling thing is that there are more and more merciless among us, those who do not even find this appalling." What is so frightening about the anti-foreigner attitude that seems to have spread throughout Germany in the early 1990s is the fact that many times the victims were long-time residents of Germany or were Germans mistaken for foreigners. In the case of Bahide Arslan, she was a long-time resident of Mölln, and her granddaughter, Yeliz, was born and raised in this North German community.

On November 23, 1992, over 10,000 people attended the funerals of the Turkish grandmother, her granddaughter, and her niece. An outpouring of sympathy and a surge of anti-violence rhetoric raced across Germany as both Turks and Germans held vigils for the stricken family. The weekend following the burials, a crowd much larger than that in Mölln gathered in Munich. Protesters carried banners and placards that were defiant of the militancy of the right-wing and railed against the lack of government action. A common phrase was, "how many children will have to fall to terror so that Bonn [Capital of the Federal Republic of Germany] will be alert?"

Before the Mölln attack, the federal agency charged with the protection of German democratic principles, *Verfassungsschutz* (Federal Office for the Protection of the Constitution), kept its distance from the right-wing militancy. Federal prosecutor Alexander von Stahl commented that, "continuous atrocities against foreigners were simply the consequences of right-wing extremism without recognizable terrorist structures."[2] Since the federal government saw no organized terrorist threat, as identified by definitions developed during the 1960s and 1970s while attempting to overcome the dangerous left-wing Red Army Faction, this office did not target the right-wing militants. Stahl went on to say that the federal courts in Karlsruhe and the government in Bonn "thought that they could keep from upgrading the political status of right-wing violence by denying it the semi-privilege of special legal treatment."[3] This approach, however, proved to be a false hope. The audacity of the neo-Nazi groups and the apparent lack of fear of the legal system that the members of these organizations portrayed quickly showed that this was the wrong way to deal with the problem. Immediately following the Mölln murders, Chancellor Helmut Kohl requested action from the *Verfassungsschutz*. Editorials flooded German newspapers as the majority made law and order the new watchword. In Frankfurt, a local radio station was less than positive about the previous efforts to control the neo-Nazis. Commenting on the Office for the Protection of the Constitution finally assuming the investigation of right-wing militants, the host of the show *"Frankfurter Rundschau"* pointed out that this "step came late, but hopefully not too late, after Karlsruhe prosecutors (federal jurists) denied their responsibility for more than a year in the face of right-wing extremist violence."[4]

Throughout Germany citizens who were outraged by the arrogance and violence of the neo-Nazis reproached the federal government officials for their apparent inaction or limited action in response to the right-wing militancy. Many people appeared to have the distinct impression that there was a growing international loss of confidence in Germany, resulting in a reduction of political credit and economic opportunities. These perceptions forced authorities at all levels to begin responding more diligently to right-wing violence. The historian Golo Mann, at age eighty-three, aptly portrayed the growing problem of right-wing violence with the comment that, "if I were fifty, I would arm myself. Trust in the state's protection clearly no longer suffices."[5] Police moved quickly and arrested suspects, many of whom were charged with murder. This was a vast change from the normal procedure of arresting perpetrators and charging them with disturbing the peace. This new attitude was viewed as a major change in the German judicial system. Rainier Voss, Chairman of the German Union of Judges, admitted that the public saw judges as inappropriately lenient. These judges became more cognizant of public opinion surrounding neo-Nazi activities, and, in many cases this led to more stringent sentences for crimes committed by the right-wing militants.

Chancellor Kohl felt the political heat as well. Protests throughout Germany forced him to take notice of the right-wing menace. His earlier efforts were not very reassuring. Kohl's denunciation of the murders at Mölln finally sounded like he was genuinely concerned. The result was that he instructed the Office for the Protection of the Constitution to investigate on the federal level and required the Attorney General to widen the interpretation of jurisdiction so that federal authorities could get more intimately involved in control of the right-wing. This, however, did not overcome the perception of many critics who still felt that Kohl wanted the German people to believe that the killings in 1992 and again in early 1993 were, in fact, ordinary crimes that local police could handle and not a terrorist activity that would threaten the German democratic structure.

Once the federal government became involved, pressure began to build on the neo-Nazi groups. Within the month following the Mölln incident, Interior Minister Rudolf Seiters banned one of the most active neo-Nazi groups, the *Nationale Liste* (NL). Although this group had no apparent connection to Mölln, it was a signal to the most virulent right-wing militant groups. In one day, police raided fifty-one houses across Germany belonging to alleged members of the NL, uncovering caches of arms and propaganda.

Over the ensuing two months, government officials at both the federal and state levels banned a total of seven neo-Nazi organizations. Three of these were especially active and potent. The *Nationalistiche Front* (NF) was banned on

November 27, 1992. This group was organized in 1985 in Bielefeld, and by 1992 it was said to have around 130 active members. The NF claimed to be a national revolutionary organization and was led by Meinholf Schoenborn. They supported the ideological ideas presented by the Strasser brothers in the early years of the NSDAP. This particular group was known for their militancy and their stockpiling of weapons and ammunition. Although small in number, the members were very active in the Nordrhein-Westphalia area of western Germany. Following banning, most of the membership joined other existing neo-Nazi groups in the region.

On December 10, 1992, federal authorities banned the group *Deutsche Alternative* (DA). The DA was founded in Bremen on May 3, 1989. This group called themselves the "National Protest Party," which was to lead the political power center of the "Imperial Loyal German-Alternative Opposition." After 1990, the DA shifted most of its activities to the eastern states, primarily in the Cottbus region of Brandenburg. Frank Huebner, twenty-six years old, led this active neo-Nazi organization that claimed approximately 350 members by 1992, with branches in Bremen, Brandenburg, Sachsen, Rheinland-Pfalz, and Berlin. Their basic ideology revolved around racial issues. Many of the followers joined the National Democratic Party (NPD) immediately following the banning.

The third major group that the federal authorities banned was the *Nationale Offensive* (NO). This organization was founded on July 3, 1990, in Augsburg, Bavaria. Originally made up of disgruntled *Freiheitliche Deutsche Arbeiterpartei* (FAP) members, the *Nationale Offensive* became more radical during 1991 and 1992. Led by thirty-one year old Michael Swierczek, this group boasted 100 members in 1991 and 140 in 1992. This growth came at the expense of other neo-Nazi groups and occurred mostly in the eastern German state of Sachsen. An aggressive propaganda source, the *Nationale Offensive* sponsored numerous events where they included such rightists as David Irving, a British revisionist historian and writer, as the primary speakers. This organization supported an ideology that blended anti-foreigner with racially motivated hate. In addition, they supported the historical revisionist view that the Holocaust did not actually occur. Their reputation led to banning on December 22, 1992. Thirty members' homes located in seven states were searched. Police confiscated propaganda, organizational documents, and computer disks.

Another two right-wing extremist organizations were placed under surveillance. The best know was the *Freiheitliche Deutsche Arbeiterpartei*, commonly referred to as the FAP. This group was organized in 1979 by Martin Pape. During the early 1980s, the FAP increased its membership rapidly, but it also began to lose members to other factions. In 1988, a power struggle for leadership occurred between Friedhelm Busse and Jürgen Mosler, resulting in

Busse becoming the head of an organization that was fraught with division. By 1992, the FAP only boasted a mere 150 members who were diversely located in Berlin, Hamburg, Niedersachsen, Nordrhein-Westfalen, and Bavaria. The group's smaller size and its less violent approach to supporting its platform saved this organization from being banned in 1992, but marked it for continued observation. The FAP ideology also was based on the Nazi Party program of the 1920s, which incorporated the Strasser brothers' concept of "People's Socialism." The FAP thesis called for the participation of labor in production and the confiscation of capital from entrepreneurs who took advantage of the average worker. Just as the Strasser's argued, the postwar neo-Nazi ideologist in the FAP placed emphasis on the need to insure that the worker received more recognition and that unemployment was best fought with job availability and social service programs that supported the worker. This particular ideology proved to be more palatable to officials than racially motivated concepts, yet the fact that the FAP tended to emulate Nazi ideals insured that they would be watched closely.

The government's banning of neo-Nazi groups was only a part of the solution. State and federal measures to curb the rising neo-Nazi movement did not end the attacks on cemeteries. Violence was reported daily, as right-wing militants grew more brazen. Banning proved to be only a temporary solution, oftentimes only lasting for a few days. Banned groups quickly reorganized and renamed themselves, pursuing the same activities and espousing the same ideology under a new name. This wanton disregard for authority, coupled with a xenophobia in the general public, allowed the continuation of violence against foreigners, asylum seekers, Jews, and, as time went on, Germans themselves.

Government efforts to control the neo-Nazi groups in 1992 sent differing signals to the right-wing extremists. Wilhelm Heitmayer, a social scientist at the University of Bielefeld, argued that the "crackdown has the misleading effect of reinterpreting the attacks as being those of a few criminals on the periphery."[6] Similarly, the Allansbach Institute supported a thesis that there were greater problems associated with the growth of right-wing militancy. This organization conducted a survey which identified that sixteen percent of the respondents in the West German states and fifteen percent in the eastern states showed sympathy for those who attacked asylum seekers.[7] Additionally, one-third of the German youths queried were openly anti-foreigner and one-quarter of the Germans asked were inclined to agree with the slogan "foreigners out."[8]

The year 1992 proved to be a year that right-wing violence became daily news. It was marked by an increase in extreme right-wing violence, with over 74 percent more acts of violence than in the previous year, the year of unification.

Young men who were unemployed and who tended to be frustrated with the inability to obtain meaningful employment and young factory workers appeared to dominate the statistics for violent activities. Those who most often were involved in violent acts were in the eighteen to thirty year old range. Interestingly, the demographics showed that the participants over the three years following unification seemed to age. As the post-unification period matured, activists in greater numbers were associated with a group ranging from twenty-one to thirty years of age, making a change from the earlier youth-dominated scene to one that clearly was becoming an adult activity with far more ominous consequences. (See Table 5.1.) The following incidents were a testament to the open brutality that became rampant during 1992.

TABLE 5.1
Acts of Right-Wing Violence and Ages of Participants

Ages	1991	1992	1993
Under 18	21.2%	23.9%	16.8%
18-20	47.8%	43.3%	39.1%
21-30	28.3%	29.9%	36.5%
31-40	2.2%	2.5%	4.9%
40 Plus	0.5%	0.4%	2.7%

Dragomir Christinel, an eighteen-year-old Rumanian, was assaulted at an asylum house in Saal near Rostock and beaten to death on March 14, 1992. The assailants were part of a neo-Nazi group of about forty participants.

Gustav Schneeclaus, a fifty-three-year-old German, was beaten to death in Buxtehude, Niedersachsen, on March 18, 1992. The perpetrators, young skinheads, claimed that Schneeclaus had called Hitler a criminal.

Ingo Finnern, age thirty-one, was a homeless person who was pushed into the water at the Flensburg, Schleswig-Holstein, port and was drowned. The neo-Nazi's motive was that Finnern remarked that he was a gypsy.

Nguyen Van Tui, a twenty-nine-year-old Vietnamese student, was stabbed by a skinhead while traveling on the Berlin Strassenbahn on April 25, 1992.

Torsten Lambrecht, a twenty-three-year-old gardener, was attacked by neo-Nazis on May 9, 1992, in Madgeburg, Sachsen-Anhalt, and died from a cracked skull.

Emil Wendland, a fifty-year-old homeless man, was brutally beaten by neo-Nazis in Neuruppen, Brandenburg, on July 1, 1992.

Sadri Berisha, a fifty-five-year-old Albanian, was beaten to death in a workhouse in Ostfeldern, Baden-Württemberg, by a group of skinheads on July 8, 1992.

Klaus Dieter Klein, another homeless man, was knocked down and literally kicked to death by right-wing militants in Bad Breisig, Rheinland-Pfalz, on August 1, 1992.

Ireneusz Szyderski, a Polish seasonal worker, aged twenty-four, was brutally beaten at a disco in Stotternheim, Thyringen, on August 3, 1992. He died from his injuries soon after being hospitalized.

Günter Schwannicke, a fifty-eight-year-old homeless person, was murdered by two skinheads who were members of a German Ku Klux Klan organization on August 29, 1992, in Berlin.

On November 7, 1992, Rolf Schulze, a homeless man in Potsdam, was beaten and set afire.

Karl-Hans Rohn, a fifty-three-year-old sales representative, was kicked to death by skinheads in Wuppertal, Nordrhein-Westfalen, on November 13, 1992. The assailants said they killed Rohn for calling them Nazi pigs during a political discussion. They drove his body to the Dutch border and dumped it into a field.

NOTES

1. Ingo Hasselbach, "How Nazis Are Made," *The New Yorker* (January 8, 1996), 48.

2. *Süddeutsche Zeitung* (November 24, 1992).

3. Ibid.

4. Daniel Benjamin, "Cracking Down On The Right," *Time* (December 14, 1992), 43.

5. Ibid.

6. Ibid., 44.

7. Ibid.

8. Ibid.

6

The Apex

Anti-Semitism was always present in postwar Germany, but until recently I believed that the law would protect me.
—Tony Abraham Merin, Babenhausen, *The Stars and Stripes*, September, 10, 1993

Police authorities in Baden-Württemberg, as well as in other states, began to develop a more definitive understanding of the neo-Nazi organizations by 1993. One such official, Hans Jürgen Ladinek, a member of the Ludwigshafen criminal police, became well known as a specialist dealing with the local right-wing militants. His peers claimed that he "knew as much as any cop in Germany about what turns bored or bitter or disappointed boys into killers who crack Turks and set refugees on fire." Ladinek came to the conclusion that "there is no way to recover these kids."

Although the neo-Nazi activities during 1992 were some of the most vicious and arbitrary in postwar German history, the militants became far more sophisticated than at any time in the postwar period in 1993. The neo-Nazis infiltrated left-wing groups far more frequently. The use of computers became widespread as names of opponents and innocents alike were stored on disks under listings such as "shoot on sight." These disks, confiscated from the National Alternative (NA) leadership, included telephone numbers, addresses, and physical descriptions that were classified into categories ranging from political opponents to types of people who were to be "shot on sight." These new methods using advanced technology were only a glimpse of the increasing instances of coordination of activities and communications between the neo-Nazi groups throughout Germany. Car telephones, cellular phones, and computer modems insured a fairly secure system of bringing these diverse groups together for common efforts.

Computer technology also was used to spread propaganda among the vulnerable youth. Programs for computer games were developed in 1993 that showed the glorification of war and nationalism. In addition, each game focused on racism and used ample numbers of Nazi symbols. Government offices tracking this new phenomenon identified over fifty programs that were being used throughout Germany which were produced by organizations such as the "Anti-Negro German Association" and "Adolf Hitler Software, LTD." The CD ROM title "Castle Wolfenstein" also was introduced during this year, providing one of the most aggressive games that incorporated illegal symbols and racist propaganda.

Neo-Nazi regional networking became far more apparent during 1993. In Baden-Württemburg, a number of small extremist organizations and splinter groups began to develop closer ties through sports days and party conventions. Computer e-mail became the preferred means of communication. All of these attempts were designed to develop a stronger unified base for neo-Nazis throughout the Baden-Württemberg region.

Outside influences also took advantage of these efforts to unify. The Ku Klux Klan from the United States began opening lines of communication through the use of propaganda, personal visits, and providing rituals that could be incorporated into the growing right-wing militant movement. The Klan was, however, unable to export the total KKK movement to Germany because of numerous differences and different priorities. They were able to provide a common ground of interest that set a precedent for future potential right-wing opportunities.

A less sophisticated, but ultimately proven means of circulating neo-Nazi hate literature was introduced during this third year following unification. Teenagers were seen reading crude comic books that were produced by right-wing extremist presses. These booklets demanded a "pure" Germany that was free of foreign "filth." Right-wing militants prowled city and village streets plastering swastika stickers on poles and walls or spraying anti-Semitic graffiti on walkways and overpasses. Underground rock concerts and neo-Nazi rallies, where young people wore SS arm-bands and waved Nazi banners, became far more prevalent. During 1993, the neo-Nazi movement seemed to gain a far more popular momentum and appeared to be swirling out of control.

Public and international pressures to contain the right-wing extremists forced the federal government to focus on the various groups. The media accused

German justice officials of being far more lenient with young neo-Nazis at the federal and state levels than with left-wing radicals. Records indicated that right-wing militants tended to get much lighter sentences, often with only probation. Federal and state level judicial offices did not maintain a central record of the sentencing of neo-Nazis, which made it difficult to ascertain the true overall impact of the right-wing violence throughout Germany. Researchers found that only about one-third of the skinhead crimes were ever sent to trial.[1] Those who were tried and convicted received remarkably light sentencing for the crimes committed. Local court records showed that this was a direct result of many of the defendants being tried as minors rather than adults or having committed the crime while under the influence of alcohol. Both of these defenses insured far lighter sentences than would normally be expected for the mayhem and brutality associated with the activities that resulted in their being arrested.

Public perceptions continued to hamper the local and federal governments' efforts to control the right-wing. Four states, Brandenburg, Mecklenburg-Vorpommern, Hessen, and Hamburg, provided approximately $240,000 from state cultural funds to subsidize a film entitled *Beruf Neonazis* (*Profession Neo-Nazi*), which was designed to expose neo-Nazi falsehoods. Unfortunately, many critics perceived this film as an effort to legitimize, rather than discredit, the local neo-Nazis. They argued that too much time was given to Bela Ewald Althans, a Munich neo-Nazi, who gave his biased views about the Holocaust, and not enough time was given to counter those comments by divulging the provision of the true historical facts.

The neo-Nazi movement showed a new and foreboding lethality during the first few months of 1993. From January 1 through the end of May, 783 non-Germans were victims of racist attacks by right-wing militants. During that time, the neo-Nazis were directly tied to four murders. Right-wing militant violence against all foreigners escalated seventy-four percent over the same period of the previous year. (See Table 6.1.)

By August 30, 1993, the number of violent attacks recorded in the state of Baden-Württemberg was at 546. During the month of June alone, a total of 173 incidents were reported. Violence in this state increased over 100 percent compared to the entire previous year. The neo-Nazis were specifically identified as having been directly involved in a total of 223 of those acts of violence. These early 1993 neo-Nazi incidents included two murders, forty arson and bomb attacks, sixty-eight threats of violence, and over 100 other types of violent acts. Baden-Württemberg officials estimated that these activities were directly associated with approximately 600 known neo-Nazis who lived in the state.

By the end of the year, government officials linked over 4,800 attacks to neo-Nazis since the unification. There were twenty-six people killed during these confrontations,with seventeen murdered during 1993 alone. Although government statistics showed a decline in neo-Nazi groups in Germany from 1992 to 1993, from eighty-two to seventy-seven, and a decline in membership from 6,400 to 5,600, viciousness associated with violent incidents took a dramatic jump.

TABLE 6.1
Neo-Nazi Violence Against Foreigners

	1992	1993	1994
Attempted Murders	6	20	8
Bombings	11	3	1
Arson	656	284	80
Terrorism	*	36	27
Bodily Harm	585	727	494
Prop. Damage	1019	539	250
Total	2277	1609	860

* Acts of Right-Wing terrorism were not tabulated before 1993.

Interestingly, the attacks against foreigners decreased by thirty percent between 1992 and 1993, and the violence committed against countrymen increased by seventy-two percent. The neo-Nazis were moving away from their favored target, the *Ausländer*, and began jeopardizing German nationals who disagreed with neo-Nazi ideology, were identified as Jewish, were suspected leftists, or who were perceived to oppose right-wing militant activities.

Attacks against left-wing groups also became more common, especially in the eastern states. Neo-Nazi groups identified opponents and prepared hit-lists that were available on computer networks and through publications. Anti-Semitism once again became a fad among many of the right-wing militant organizations. More attacks against Jewish cemeteries occurred in 1993 than were perpetrated by the Nazis between 1929 and 1933.[2] In Worms during 1993, right-wing vandals viciously attacked the oldest Jewish cemetery in Europe, resulting in the desecration of over 500 gravestones. Neo-Nazi hoodlums spray-painted swastikas and the SS symbol on 100 of the gravestones. Ignatz Bubis, Chairman of the Central Council of Jews in Germany, was appalled at the destruction, saying that "Nazis under Hitler seldom desecrated Jewish cemeteries (except in Frankfurt)."[3]

TABLE 6.2
Neo-Nazi Violence Against Other Germans

	1992	1993	1994
Attempted Murders	10	3	2
Bombings	3	0	0
Arson	43	27	20
Terrorism	*	57	22
Bodily Harm	173	172	131
Prop. Damage	133	364	454
Total	362	623	629

Following the attacks in Worms, neo-Nazis struck again in Sachsenhausen, where a Jewish memorial to the Holocaust victims was enshrined. The memorial itself was desecrated with swastikas and anti-Semitic graffiti. The guest book also was vandalized.

Right-wing militants brought anti-Semitism to life throughout Germany following unification. Tony Abraham Merin, the last Jew to live in Babenhausen, decided in 1993 that he had to leave his home because of threats and insults from local rightists. He commented to a local reporter about his decision by saying that "anti-Semitism was always present in postwar Germany, but until recently [1993] he [Merin] believed that the law would protect him. That feeling is gone".[4]

The increasing militancy opened a new chapter in right-wing history during 1993. Neo-Nazi aggression and open hostility against not only foreigners, but also their own countrymen, became far more commonplace. No longer in the background of German radicalism, these modern-day Nazis caused many Germans and foreigners alike to realize the danger posed by such extremists in the newly unified Germany during 1993. These radicals became a force that had to be dealt with quickly and uncompromisingly before their poison spread too far.

The violence associated with the 1993 incidents provided excellent news material. The number of acts that were directly related to the neo-Nazi groups during the year made it difficult to stay abreast of the incidents. On February 20, 1993, a confrontation between right-wing militants and leftists set the stage for the rest of the year. During the evening, a driver for a heavy-metal music band was beaten by seven right-wing youths in the town of Hoyerswerda. The victim sustained serious injuries and died six days later. The result was a heightening of tensions between right-wing militants and left-wing radicals in the community.

On March 9, 1993, in the small town of Mühlheim an der Ruhr, a fifty-six-year-old Turkish man was attacked by two twenty-one-year-old men with a gas pistol. This victim was subjected to superficial wounds from the pistol and was insulted with comments such as "asylum seeker and shit Turk." The two young men were so abusive and aggressive that the victim collapsed from heart failure and died.

During that same month, neo-Nazis in Potsdam injured three patrons in a bar fight. Approximately fifteen neo-Nazi skinheads used bottles, chairs, and table legs to beat three university students at a local club. A twenty-three-year-old student was rushed to the hospital with an apparent fractured skull; the other two victims received minor injuries in the melee. Police arrested eight skinheads for assault and battery.

By the end of May, neo-Nazi violence was escalating to far more dangerous proportions. On May 29, five Turkish immigrants were killed in a fire set by neo-Nazis in Solingen, Nordrhein-Westfalen. This was considered to be the deadliest attack on foreigners in Germany since the Nazi era. Five perpetrators were arrested and charged with arson, including a sixteen-year-old student, a twenty year old military draftee, and a twenty-three-year-old who was unemployed. This arson attack took the lives of two women and three children, galvanizing a movement against right-wing violence within the foreign community and forcing government officials to become more actively involved in solving the right-wing "problem." It took two and one-half years before the assailants were finally sentenced.

On October 12, 1995, the courts in Düsseldorf found four of the activists guilty of murder. The oldest defendant, Markus Gartmann, twenty-five years old, faced the possibility of life in prison. The five-judge panel, however, only sentenced him to fifteen years. Felix Koehnen, eighteen years old; Christian Buchholz, twenty-two; and Christian Reher, nineteen, were tried as juveniles. These three neo-Nazis were each given the maximum ten year sentences allowed under the juvenile laws.

Christian Reher was the only defendant to confess and continue to support his confession throughout the entire trial. Markus Gartmann confessed initially, but retracted his statements over the eighteen months that the trial wore on. Koehnen responded to the sentencing by screaming "you swine, I am innocent."[5] He went on to threaten suicide.

After the sentences were handed down, a mostly Turkish crowd outside the courthouse showed disgust for the seemingly light sentences. One demonstrator, Suat Kolsuz, who had lived in Germany for over sixteen years, commented "the sentences show that Germany has not learned from its Fascist Hitler past."[6]

While local groups of neo-Nazis were flexing their muscles, a growing international right-wing movement was evolving. On June 19 and 20, 1993, French and German neo-Nazis gathered in Vellexon, France. This was the beginning of a series of multinational right-wing extremist meetings that built a common alliance between previously divergent groups.

Pressures on state and federal officials to gain control of the neo-Nazi movement accelerated during mid-Summer, particularly following the Solingen murders. The states of Bavaria, Baden-Württemberg, and Nordrhein-Westfalen banned the neo-Nazi groups the *Nationaler Block* (NB) on June 11, 1993, the *Heimattreue Vereinigung Deutschlands* (HVD) on July 14, 1993, and the smaller *Freundeskreis für Deutschland* (FFD) on September 2, 1993. The banning of these groups was predicated on the accusation that they all showed excessive hostility toward Jews and conducted racist agitation against refugees.

The HVD (Patriotic Union of Germany), in particular, was identified as a virulent racist, anti-foreigner organization that threatened the German Constitution and advocated Nazism. As of the date of banning, officials estimated that there were sixty hard-core members of this group. On July 14, 1993, police searched twenty-four houses belonging to HVD members and found weapons, Nazi uniforms, written propaganda, and computer software. Confiscated documents indicated that this group enjoyed close connections throughout Europe and particularly with a group called *Heimattreue Vereinigung Elsap* (HVE) located in the Alsace region between Germany and France. These two organizations were found to have conducted regular combined meetings throughout 1992 and early 1993, as well as paramilitary exercises in the Alsace forests.

During this same period of time, the federal government continued monitoring the *Freiheitlichen Deutschen Arbeiterpartei* (FAP) for possible banning. Officials in Nordrhein-Westfalen raided five sites and confiscated neo-Nazi materials. It appeared that the FAP was becoming a potential target for government action against the larger neo-Nazi organizations.

German officials were realizing the extent of both the national and international neo-Nazi network. The Chief of German Internal Security, Eckart Werthebach, declared in August 1993, that the "neo-Nazis have taken steps to form a national network." The Office for the Protection of the Constitution, *Verfassungsschutz*, reported that this was the first time that "action alliances" among previously splintered neo-Nazi groups had emerged, and, therefore, "these are the first steps toward a network."[7]

The neo-Nazi network showed its strength on August 14, 1993, in the town of Fulda, Hessen. Over 500 neo-Nazis, including British, French, and Dutch, gathered for three hours to mark the anniversary of Rudolf Hess's death in 1987. The participants unfurled banners saying "In Remembrance of Rudolf Hess" and shouted right-wing slogans for three hours admonishing foreigners "to get out of Germany." The primary speakers included the British nationalist, John Peacock, aged fifty-one, and Claude Cornilleau, a fifty-seven-year-old known French neo-Nazi.

The demonstration began in the neighboring town of Thürinen, but the local officials banned the activity at the last moment. The participants then loaded into six buses and fifty cars after informing the police that they were going to two alternate locations. Once on the road, the buses and cars drove directly to Fulda, thereby outwitting the unprepared police. Ultimately, the Fulda demonstration was monitored by eighty policemen who remained distant from the crowds. On the outskirts of Fulda, approximately 140 police kept left-wing counter-demonstrators from entering the town. Critical responses to the police procedures were rapid. Police officials drew the ire of many for their failure to halt the neo-Nazi demonstration. Some leftist leaders claimed that the police used a double standard by allowing the right-wing activities to be conducted in Fulda, while at the same time insuring that the counter-demonstrators were kept at bay. The police argued that they were preventing violence by keeping the two sides separated and only monitoring the demonstration.

Vandalism continued unabated during August 1993. Right-wing youths tampered with an exhibit set up in Nuremberg in an area below the *Zeppelin-Tribune Newspaper* offices that provided information about the *Reichspartei* bannister. The guest book was found to have been defaced with such scribbling as "I was here! Only my Führer was no longer here," and "In spite of the imperialistic war against our pledge to Germany, in spite of lies and anti-German talk, I say proudly: I am glad to be German, All for Germany."[8]

Police raided a "grill-fest" on August 28, 1993, that was being held in support of a previously banned right-wing militant organization. Participants included young people from both Heidelberg and Karlsruhe, in the state of Baden-Württemberg. Twenty-seven activists were arrested at the restaurant and another thirty-four were taken into custody at the train station. Officials found sufficient evidence to suggest that the neo-Nazis in this group were receiving financial support from well-off retired Nazis. There were also suspicions that members of the Republikaner Party may have provided some funds, which, of course, was disavowed by the party leadership.

In late August, German neo-Nazis again met with compatriots from a number of European countries and North America in the town of Diksmuidi, located in the West Flanders area of Belgium. Following these meetings was a string of incidents propagated against foreigners. On August 31, 1993, 100 refugees fled from a burning asylum shelter in the town of Detmold, located in western Germany. Officials determined that the cause of the blaze was attributed to right-wing extremist arsonists. One day earlier, in Idar-Oberstein, Germany, an Afghanistan immigrant's grocery store was fire-bombed. The perpetrators printed swastikas and the slogan "foreigners out" on the exterior walls of the store using black enamel paint.

This spate of arson in August forced additional responses from local authorities. In the state of Brandenburg, officials banned public displays of the *Reichskriegflagge*, the former German imperial war flag that had become a neo-Nazi symbol. Authorities said that the reasons for banning the flag were because it now symbolized neo-Fascism, xenophobia, and racism, and therefore was a rallying symbol for anti-constitutional forces. The flag itself incorporated an eagle and iron cross against a background of black, red, and white. Traditionally, this particular flag was used by the German navy during World War II. By adopting the imperial flag, the neo-Nazis incorporated a nationalist symbol that carried a sense of nostalgia among many Germans.

In mid-September, an incident occurred in Griesheim, just outside of Frankfurt, that brought right-wing militancy directly to the doorsteps of Americans living in Germany. Patrick Patterson, a nineteen year old whose father was American and mother was German, was confronted at a local fest in a disco by a group of young neo-Nazis. Patterson, who was dark-skinned, was jostled, shoved, and called "nigger" by two young men inside the disco.[9] Escaping to the outside, Patterson was again attacked by three more youths. As if this was not bad enough, police who were dispatched to the scene did not interfere immediately, but allowed the activity to continue for a short time. The police chief, when queried as to the reason for his men not stepping in immediately, remarked that "those five young men shouting 'Sieg Heil' didn't make them neo-Nazis," therefore, the need to take immediate action was not necessary.[10]

Also during September, two fourteen-year-old boys were charged in the eastern town of Frankfurt an der Oder with smashing tombstones and painting swastikas on Jewish headstones in a graveyard located in the village of Wriezen. Authorities all over Germany were responding to a seemingly endless string of right-wing violence and mischief. No region seemed immune to these activities.

Early Fall provided a good time for additional gatherings of European neo-Nazis. From September 26 to September 30, 1993, the Austrian neo-Nazi group *Deutschen Kulturgemeinschaft* (DKG) hosted a "guest week" for right-wing militants from the German city of Nauemburg in Sachsen-Anhalt. And then, on October 2, 1993, Dr. Frey, leader of the right-wing organization DVU (German People's Union), took part in a conference in Passau that supported neo-Nazi programs in conjunction with Austrian and South Tyrolian right-wing extremists. This particular conference was notable because of the support provided by the Russian right-wing politician, Zirinovsky.

The anniversary of German unification on October 3, 1993, provided the opportunity for new right-wing activities. This day became something of a neo-Nazi holiday. In the town of Hünxe, a group of teenage skinheads got drunk, assembled two molotov cocktails, and threw them at the residence of a local Lebanese family. The family had only lived in this community for two years. When authorities tracked down the skinheads, they were surprised to find that the father of one of the youths had decorated the bar in the basement of his home with Nazi paraphernalia and had a large party every year in celebration of Hitler's birthday.

October ended on a sour note, as once again Americans were directly subjected to the militancy of the neo-Nazis. Duncan Kennedy, a U.S. luge racer who was training in the eastern German town of Oberdorf for the Olympics, was beaten outside of a local bar by fifteen young men identified by police as local neo-Nazis. Duncan was protecting a teammate, Robert Pipkins, who was a black American athlete. Pipkins was being taunted by monkey noises and shouts of "nigger out."[11] Duncan placed himself between the neo-Nazis and Pipkins, trying to disengage the activists. The German youths then began beating Duncan. The entire village of Oberdorf was dismayed with this neo-Nazi act of violence and issued a formal apology to the U.S. luge team, saying that the youths involved were from neighboring villages. Charges were brought against the main perpetrators, many of whom received sentences for limited jail time and then probation. This incident increased the discomfiture of some Americans living and working in Germany. A German politician with the Christian Democratic Union (CDU) said that the attack on the U.S. luge racer proved that the "current [German] laws are not tough enough to deter violent neo-Nazis who have carried out more than 1,500 attacks this year [1993]."[12]

The year 1993 seemed to be a year of unending neo-Nazi activities that seriously pressed the local authorities and forced the state and federal law agencies and governments to emphasize the need for more control. Banning neo-Nazi groups became the favored means of obtaining that objective. Adjudication of crimes resulted in increasingly more stringent sentences. Identification of neo-

Nazi hangouts were made quickly. Businesses in cities such as Nürnberg that were known to cater to neo-Nazis were placed under observation. Included on this list were such popular eating and drinking establishments throughout Germany as the Moltenkistle-Pilstube, located at Siemenstrasse 24 in Nürnberg; the U-Bahn Quick at the main train station in Fürth; the Disco Trend in Schwabach; the Münchener Kindl, located at Luitpoldstrasse 54 in Erlangen; the Grüner Baum at Erlangenstrasse 12, in Kalchreuth; the Melody Sam, located at Burgstallerweg 2, in Herzogenaurach; and the Wölkerbraue, at Oberbrauhausgasse 4, in Höchstadt an der Aisch. All of these businesses, located throughout Germany, seemed to defer to the young right-wing militants, giving them a place to gather, drink beer, and plan their activities.

Throughout the year, neo-Nazis in Berlin distributed pamphlets listing hundreds of local politicians, judges, lawyers, and professors who were targeted for "final elimination" once the neo-Nazis gained power. A television station, ARO, found that these pamphlets were being distributed nationally, and that many lists contained names and addresses of those to be "suppressed" and designated for "final elimination" because of their opposition to the existing neo-Nazi groups. This national approach to identifying opponents led German authorities to the conclusion that there were signs that the many neo-Nazi groups very possibly were coalescing into a single movement.

Chancellor Kohl, feeling increased political pressures, again promised on September 13, 1993, to "crack down" on the neo-Nazis. It was becoming evident that bad publicity was staining Germany's international image. Kohl described the neo-Nazis of Germany as a "small minority that had hurt Germany's image abroad."[13] In addition, the ruling political party, the Christian Democratic Union (CDU), pledged as an organization to not cooperate with the right-wing extremist parties, thereby weakening the political opportunities of the fringe extremist organizations and indirectly the political fortunes of the neo-Nazis. These efforts directly contributed to the reduction in 1994 of neo-Nazi influence and activity. It did not, however, stop the violence and activities of the stronger neo-Nazi groups within Germany and in bordering countries. The result was the movement of the organizations north into Denmark, where laws were more liberal, particularly those dealing with publishing.

NOTES

1. Jane Kramer, "Neo-Nazis: A Chaos In The Head," *The New Yorker* (June 14, 1993), 69.

2. *The Stars and Stripes* (September 15, 1993).

3. *The Stars and Stripes* (September 1, 1993).

4. *The Stars and Stripes* (September 10,1993).

5. "Germans Found Guilty In Deadly Firebombing," *The Stars and Stripes* (October 14, 1993).

6. Ibid.

7. *The Stars and Stripes* (September 1, 1993).

8. *The Stars and Stripes* (August 23, 1993).

9. *The Stars and Stripes* (September 10, 1993).

10. Ibid.

11. *The Stars and Stripes* (October 29, 1993).

12. Ibid.

13. *The Stars and Stripes* (September 15, 1993).

7

The Decline

Unwanted listeners are hereby informed that this connection is for friends and is not public...Heil Hitler.

—Neo-Nazi telephone message, *The Stars and Stripes*, August 27, 1994

Following two years of especially brutal right-wing militant violence, police officials throughout Germany braced for the new year of 1994. Finally it appeared that the government's concentrated efforts would slow or even stop the violence from neo-Nazis and skinheads. The year was, in fact, marked with a noticeable decrease in violence, assumably associated with the actions taken at both the federal and state levels to subdue the right-wing militants. This is not to say that neo-Nazis totally acquiesced to the increasing pressures. Almost 1,500 acts of violence were perpetrated during 1994 compared to over 2,200 in 1993. Important in these statistics is that the number of violent attacks against foreigners actually dropped forty-seven percent, whereas the number of attacks against countrymen increased slightly. Therefore, the numerical differences in incidents between 1993 and 1994 can be tied directly to a change in targets. Some of this can be attributed to government involvement, but some also can be associated with a clear effort from the foreign communities to protect themselves from the neo-Nazis and skinheads. This, however, did not stop the most violent militants. Although the neo-Nazi groups were less visible in many parts of Germany, there were still those who continued to stalk and brutalize people who did not support right-wing militant activities.

Eastern Germany seemed to carry the brunt of the violence in 1994. In Floessberg, a town approximately fifty miles west of Dresden, fifteen young neo-Nazis were arrested for allegedly breaking into a youth club in early March and beating eleven patrons with baseball bats and rubber clubs. The attackers apparently identified the location as a hangout for left-wing supporters, therefore making the club, and any who were unfortunate enough to be present, a perfect target for violence against a perceived enemy of the right-wing. The police searched the homes of the alleged conspirators, all of whom ranged from eighteen to twenty-six years of age, confiscating baseball bats and neo-Nazi propaganda.

This early 1994 incident that showed a clear example of apparent disregard for other people's lives was only one example of the violence that the neo-Nazis perpetrated from unification in 1990 through the end of 1994. Over those first four years of the decade, right-wing militants killed more than thirty people and injured hundreds more, all of whom were targets because of race, nationality, differing ideology, or having suggested that they were opposed to the increasing wave of violence associated with the neo-Nazi movement.

Following the incident in Floessberg, a group of three skinheads insulted and attacked a thirty-one year old Ghanian immigrant in the city of Halle. After beating the man extensively, the neo-Nazis then kicked him out of a moving streetcar, severely injuring him. When the police interrogated the three young men, they claimed that the victim was "job competition," and that they saw him as a rival for work opportunities that German youths should have available.

Neo-Nazi activity and violence during August proved to be some of the most severe during that year. Numerous arranged memorials designed to remember those who died during World War II fueled the flames of right-wing discontent. The increased international interest in the Holocaust and official services honoring those who died in Nazi concentration camps were a prelude to the upcoming fiftieth anniversary of the end of the war. These activities set the stage for young right-wing militants to express their outrage for these efforts to remember the victims of Nazi Germany.

In early August, at the Buchenwald Concentration Camp Memorial, located outside the city of Weimar and approximately 120 miles southwest of Berlin, the Israeli Ambassador's visit was clouded by neo-Nazis shouting "Sieg Heil" and throwing stones at the participants. Approximately twenty-two neo-Nazis were organized and bussed to Buchenwald on a commercial tourist bus to disrupt an important visit that was the prelude to the fiftieth anniversary of liberation planned for the coming year.

The militants' interest in the Buchenwald memorial was the issue of whether or not reported Nazi atrocities committed during World War II in this and many other concentration camps were actually true. This question was a primary ideological issue that prevailed among the right-wing radicals. Many neo-Nazis and right-wing leaders and supporters disagreed about the validity of the Holocaust. Supported by a number of revisionists, such as the British writer David Irving, the Austrian authors Walter Ochenberger and Gerd Honsik, and Germans Dr. Max Wahl, editor of a right-wing newsletter called "Halt," Thies Christophersen, living in Denmark and editor of the quarterly news "*Die Bauernschaft,*" and Ernst Zündel, a rabid activist and propagandist who left Germany and emigrated to Canada, the neo-Nazis spread the idea that the Holocaust did not occur. They claimed that the Allies, led by the United States and Israel, planted the story to discredit Germany. Even with the overwhelming evidence provided by photographs at liberation, films that were confiscated, and personal accounts given by the survivors, the abhorrence of Hitler's terrible deeds was unacceptable to modern neo-Nazis such as Ernst Zündel and his other "sophisticated" cronies.[1]

To this revisionist group it was therefore important that a concerted effort to disrupt the activities at Buchenwald be organized and receive media attention. This particular memorial had been a major Nazi concentration camp during the 1930s and 1940s. Over 56,000 people died at Buchenwald between 1937 and 1945, each death carefully recorded. In all, the Nazis interned about 238,000 people in this infamous concentration camp, including Jews, Gypsies, Soviet prisoners-of-war, and German political prisoners. The sheer gravity of the atrocities attributed to the Nazis was something that the extreme right-wing radicals wanted minimized or forgotten.

The need to downplay the Holocaust became a major area of contention between the right-wing militants and the government. The Basic Law (German Constitution) enacted in 1949 explicitly outlawed Nazi symbols and public reference to Adolf Hitler. The judiciary had already determined that the denial of the Holocaust was in contravention of this federal constitution. The nation's highest court ruled in April 1994 that freedom of speech did not extend to neo-Nazis who claimed that the Holocaust never occurred; this overturned a lower court ruling that was made in March. In essence, an individual in Germany became subject to confinement for having the wrong view of history when it pertained to the Hitler era. During 1994, Munich authorities sentenced a number of neo-Nazi activists to prison terms for denying that the Holocaust occurred.

Outsiders were not exempt from the changing German attitudes concerning this historical aspect. David Irving, a well-known revisionist British historian and author, became persona-non-grata in Germany. For years Irving participated in right-wing forums in Germany that disputed the Holocaust. His welcome into Germany was finally withdrawn in 1994, as federal and state officials began to place pressure on the right-wing for its rhetoric and illegal activities.

By mid-Summer of 1994, government authorities were actively pursuing leads associated with the curtailment of the violent neo-Nazi culture. On August 15, two judges were released from their duties "due to long-term illness." Judges Wolfgang Mueller and Rainier Orlet appeared to have been overly sympathetic to the right-wing militant's anti-Semitic views. The judges were relieved of their positions after they had handed down a suspended sentence to Günter Deckert, the local leader of the National Democratic Party (NPD), after he publicly denied that the Holocaust occurred.

This was not the first incident of government officials showing apparent sympathy by for the right-wing militant movement. The author of an article titled *"Den Ruf lädiert,"* in the prestigious German magazine *Der Spiegel*, publicized information that West Berlin reserve police were known to have tolerated known criminals and right-wing extremists in their organization since February 1993. In another example of police collusion and empathy, twenty-seven police officers in Hamburg were suspended in September 1994 for beating foreign detainees.

The mid-August 1994 anniversary of the death of Rudolf Hess provided the opportunity for the neo-Nazis to demonstrate their continued strength. In all, police arrested twenty-four neo-Nazis in an attempt to defuse the potentially dangerous demonstrations surrounding the seventh anniversary of Hess's death. Seven youths were arrested in Wernigerode, Saxony-Anhalt, while putting up signs advertising a neo-Nazi meeting. In the state of Thüringen, where the neo-Nazi movement was considered to be particularly strong, five leading local neo-Nazis were detained. In Meeane, Saxony, six neo-Nazis were arrested for shouting "Heil Hitler" and "Sieg Heil." In addition, on August 12, police banned two neo-Nazi rallies that were part of a total of thirty demonstrations that were banned over the summer in order to try and defuse the Hess memorial. And again on August 13, police averted an attempt by six young men, ages sixteen and twenty, from desecrating the Buchenwald memorial and confiscated neo-Nazi materials that were to be distributed outside of the gates. These incidents clearly supported the thesis that the modern neo-Nazi felt impelled to use Nazi symbols of the past, in this case Rudolf Hess and the Buchenwald concentration camp, to insure some sense of continuity with history to justify their existence.

The initial post-unification years, running from 1990 through 1994, were important years for both the neo-Nazi organizations and the federal government. The right-wing militants became far more sophisticated in their tactics and in their means of organization. Becoming increasingly attached to modern technology to enhance their image, neo-Nazi groups throughout Europe became "computer literate" and developed sophisticated means of communicating through local telephone services. Utilizing telephones, right-wing militant groups were able to spread their propaganda and provide information to supporters without worrying about being subjected to direct police scrutiny. An advertised number was used which provided a recorded message that was designed to reduce outsider involvement and clarify for whom the information was given. The normal message began with, "Unwanted listeners are hereby informed that this connection is only for friends and is not public."[2] This rather obvious message then was followed by information on right-wing activities, marches, and concerts, and concluded with the farewell, "Heil, Germany."[3] This public approach of providing information was an example of the disdain that the neo-Nazis had for the laws and the governmental attempts to eliminate right-wing radicalism. In fact, this particular phone message remained active for over one and one- half years. There were an additional six numbers that provided similar formats in areas such as Berlin, Hamberg, and Nürnberg. Officials determined that this phone net was developed and managed by members of the Independent German Worker's Party, a well-known right-wing radical group that was pursuing political opportunities.[4] The chief of the Nordrhein-Westfalen *Verfassungsschutz*, Fritz Achim Baumann, characterized those involved in this means of communications as a group who were not a "bunch of inexperienced, stupid people."[5] The problem for officials who wanted to truncate the availability of these means of communications was that the right-wing militants seemed to be quite capable of officially remaining on the edge of the law in a "gray area," where groups were protected as long as they did not specifically break the law. Those right-wing members that stepped beyond the "gray area" and broke the law then became far more vulnerable to government action as the political pressures built to quash the growth of neo-Nazism in Germany.

The judicial system became more responsive to the need to punish those responsible for ever-increasing illegal activities associated with the right-wing militants. In August 1994, three neo-Nazi leaders in Berlin who had advocated violence against foreigners in the city of Magdeburg were each sentenced to up to three years in prison. Initially, the events that resulted in sentencing began in mid-May 1994, when a group of local neo-Nazis began a drunken hunt for Turkish immigrants. A riot ensued that resulted in the worst violence in 1994. The police apprehended and booked the three neo-Nazi ringleaders. The ages of these three self-proclaimed fascists ranged from twenty-one to twenty-three. They were charged with grievous breach of public order and in August were finally sentenced.

During the first week in September four neo-Nazis, called skinheads by the media, rampaged through downtown Trier, a German city near the border of Germany and Luxembourg, shouting Nazi slogans. In the process, these militant youths overturned sidewalk cafe furniture and shouted "Sieg Heil" and

"Heil Hitler." When the police officer tried to arrest the nineteen-year-old ringleader, the young hoodlum kicked the officer in the face with combat boots. This confrontation resulted in the police officer being admitted to a local hospital with a brain concussion, splintered bones in his face, and a whiplash neck injury. The perpetrator was jailed for resisting arrest and causing serious bodily harm. This apparent disregard for authority and the viciousness displayed by the neo-Nazis throughout 1993 and the summer of 1994 forced the local police officials to develop a far greater appreciation for the threat posed by the growing neo-Nazi movement.

Graph 7.1
Right-Wing Militant Violence

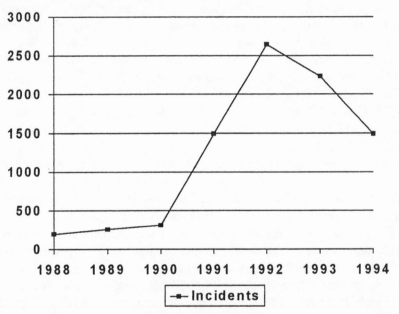

During the same week that the events in Trier unfolded, four more neo-Nazis were arrested in the area of the Sachsenhausen Concentration Camp Memorial. Once again, in a repeat of the Buchenwald incident, right-wing hooligans ranging in age from twenty-one to twenty-nine shouted "Heil Hitler" as loudly as possible and presented the Nazi salute in order to disrupt the solemnity of this most important memorial to those who died in Nazi concentration camps. Between 120,000 and 204,000 people, mostly Jews, perished in the Sachsenhausen death camp from starvation and malnutrition from 1936 to 1945. The four neo-Nazis who attempted to disrupt the anniversary of such an infamous detention center were from Berlin and a small suburb, Oberhavel. They claimed that they specifically came to Sachsenhausen to make a spectacle and gain attention. All four were arrested and charged with public incitement and for shouting banned Nazi slogans.

Graph 7.2
Right-Wing Militant Membership

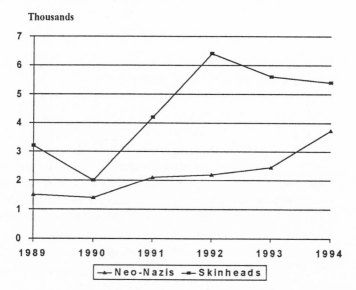

Not more than two days after the arrests, a fire was set next to the Sachsenhausen Camp Memorial in retribution. The fire gutted an abandoned Nazi-era bakery, giving notice that the militant movement was still very much alive.

This was not the first time that the Sachsenhausen Memorial was a neo-Nazi target since unification. A number of similar incidents were attempted over the preceding four years. In September 1992, a wooden barracks located inside of the memorial grounds also was destroyed by an arson attack. The right-wing militants attacked these symbols of the Nazi past in a continuing effort to discredit the memory of Nazi atrocities committed in the infamous concentration camps throughout Central Europe.

Following a particularly active month of August, the next month proved to be a period of continued violence, this time against foreigners and Jewish targets. Near the end of September, six neo-Nazis boarded a local train in Berlin and began harassing passengers by shooting needles at them through homemade blowguns. Just before midnight, the train stopped in the eastern Berlin district of Pankow, where a twenty-five year old Ghanian man, who was in Germany seeking asylum, boarded. Shortly after the victim, Katom J., boarded the train he was confronted by neo-Nazi skinheads. Six youths approached Katom with drawn switchblade knives, stabbed him several times, and then opened the doors and kicked him out of the moving train. The victim was found near Hohen Neuendorf, a railroad station northwest of Berlin. He suffered a fractured skull, numerous lacerations and knife wounds, and a crushed right foot and left calf, which were apparently the result of being run over by the train. Doctors were forced to amputate the leg and two toes on the other foot as a consequence of the injuries.

The sheer brutality of this attack and the fact that it occurred on a major mode of public transportation caused federal officials to reappraise the need for even stricter laws dealing with the neo-Nazi movement. A new crime law, designed to "get tougher" on right-wing attackers, was introduced and passed by the Bundestag, the lower house of the German Parliament. The primary purpose of this new crime law was specifically to fight neo-Nazi activities. The provisions included a maximum sentence increase from three to five years for punishments involving the causing of bodily injury. It also included an increase from three to five years for a maximum sentence resulting from charges associated with denial of the Holocaust. All neo-Nazi symbols were banned, and police officials were granted wider authority in using wiretap information. This, in essence, set aside another law that was in effect since 1945, which limited wiretap opportunities. Under this new provision, wiretap data were allowed to be passed to local police from the Federal Intelligence Service (FIS). This organization traditionally used wiretap information to track international terrorists and spies. By providing the opportunity for more direct dissemination to local authorities, the new law made it far easier to identify and track right-wing militants and their organizations.

Neo-Nazi fervor in 1994 seemed to be at its peak during September. Jewish sites became specific targets throughout Germany. In Lübeck, four youths were tried for fire-bombing a Jewish synagogue earlier in the year. Five tenants were asleep in apartments in the building when it was fire-bombed. Fortunately, all five escaped after neighbors alerted them. The perpetrators, Stefan-Marcus Westphal, aged twenty-five, Dirk Brusberg, aged twenty-two, and Niko Trapiel and Boris Holland-Moritz, both twenty, were tried for attempted murder as well as arson. The judge, Hermann Ehrich, however, refused to sentence the four for attempted murder, saying that the arsonists did not know that there was anyone inside the building. The four young men received sentences of jail terms ranging from two and one-half to four and one-half years. This was the first time that a Jewish house of worship was set afire since the Nazi years, and it readily evoked memories of the infamous Nazi pogroms.

Also during September 1994, international neo-Nazi activities became more visible. In Copenhagen, Denmark, a Danish citizen was arrested for distributing neo-Nazi pamphlets that listed over 250 opponents of the right-wing who were identified for "final solution," or more specifically, eventual death.[6] At the man's trial it was disclosed that the materials were written and printed in Germany, and then distributed through a German post office box address. The pamphlet, a fifty-page printed booklet entitled "*Einblick*" (*Insight*), included a coupon for obtaining more information on the views of the neo-Nazis.

Interestingly, Denmark became somewhat of a haven for German neo-Nazis during late 1993, because the Danish laws were far more liberal concerning the publication and distribution of various political views. In addition, the Danes were far less concerned with radicals who moved into Denmark, as long as they did not break Danish laws. However, in the case of the distribution of "*Einblick*," the government deemed that the pamphlet was inflammatory and therefore dangerous to society. Obviously, it went beyond the realm of acceptable material when it named persons to be eliminated because of opposition to a particular radical group. The Danish citizen who was arrested was presumed to be a member of Denmark's National Socialist Movement (DNSB), which was considered to be the largest right-wing extremist organization in the country in 1993 and 1994.

From January 1, 1994, through September 15, 1994, officials reported 1,000 right-wing militant attacks throughout Germany. This was an average of three incidents per day. Although seemingly an unacceptable number of attacks, the neo-Nazis were less active than in 1993. By October, neo-Nazi activities became less frequent, primarily due to government intervention. Neo-Nazi acts of violence, in fact, decreased from 1,737 to 1,127, approximately thirty-five percent, from January to October 1994 over the same period the previous year.

Although neo-Nazi activities began to decline after September, the most militant groups continued to show a presence throughout Germany. By November, however, the police faced a new problem. A neo-Nazi meeting held in Stuttgart drew a large number of participants to the Weilimdorg district. Right-wing militants from Baden-Württemberg, Bavaria, Saarland, and the Rhineland-Pfalz gathered to organize a new and more centralized neo-Nazi organization. The main organizer, a forty-seven year old man, became violent when police attempted to break up the demonstration. When officers attempted to arrest him, he pulled a knife and brazenly stabbed an officer in the hand. This act released a flurry of anti-police activities, with other demonstrators hurdling beer bottles and glasses at the police line. The only way that the police could react was to barricade the demonstration area until the right-wing demonstrators quieted down. The aftermath of the riot showed the vulnerability of local police.

Nine officers were injured and 197 demonstrators were arrested, including some women and youths. Most of those arrested were detained for one night and released the next morning after their identification was verified. The size and resulting militancy of this demonstration clarified the potential power that the neo-Nazi movement was accumulating.

By mid-November, the Ministry of the Interior deemed it necessary once again to ban a major neo-Nazi group. On November 10, 1994, the organization Viking Youth (WJ) was officially banned throughout Germany. This group was the oldest right-wing militant organization in Germany, having been organized in 1952, and was considered by many to have been the successor to the Hitler Youth. Although they were never linked directly to violence, officials claimed that the membership, most of whom were adults, and numbering about 400 active members, were in violation of the German Basic Law (Constitution), which prohibited actions that endangered the democratic principles of postwar Germany. Using Article Twenty-One, which authorized the Minister of the Interior to ban nationally active groups that were determined to be a danger to democracy, authorities banned the Viking Youth. It was determined that the basic premise of the Viking Youth was the commitment of its members to overthrow the constitution, using violence, if necessary. Many neo-Nazis considered the loophole in the Basic Law to be Article 146, which declared that, once Germany was united, the Basic Law would be replaced with a constitution. They claimed that the "Basic Law shall lose validity on that day when the constitution freely chosen by the German people enters into force."[7] In place of the Basic Law and democratic government this movement supported the creation of a National Socialist state with racist and anti-Semitic beliefs that included forcing Jews to wear yellow stars and sterilization of people who the extremists considered "inferior beings." Their activities included paramilitary training and an aggressive indoctrination program targeted at youths and children. The Viking Youth leadership encouraged members to serve in the German Bundeswehr in order to develop their physical abilities and to receive free weapons training.[8]

During recent years there were a number of documented instances where the Viking Youth conducted full-scale military-style exercises, drawing participants from throughout Germany. Officials described the Viking Youth as an organization that had close ties to the neo-Nazi scene and the National Democratic Party of Germany (NPD), the old stalwart of right-wing extremist politics in western Germany.

Interestingly, during 1994 there were fifty-four registered cases of right-wing extremist activities in the German military. Of these fifty-four cases, thirty-five were charges stemming from the service member making statements that were considered inflammatory right-wing extremism, and nineteen were instances of the individuals using or displaying prohibited Nazi or neo-Nazi symbols. Another five cases of suspected right-wing extremist activities were associated with nineteen service members who were identified as possibly being involved in right-wing violence. In comparison, during 1993 there were only seventeen cases that implicated a total of twenty-six German military members who were tied to right-wing extremism.

Following government outlawing of the Viking Youth, police raided a number of the members' homes. They seized knives, uniforms, bank documents, computer disks, Nazi song books, propaganda, and bank accounts. Led by the thirty year old Wolfram Nahrath, called by his members "federal Führer," this Fascist organization maintained a link between members of neo-Nazi groups that were previously banned, supplying an effective nodal for the growing national and international neo-Nazi network. Nahrath's Berlin apartment was a key target for the police raids, which resulted in the confiscation of money belonging to the organization. Government officials considered the banning and subsequent confiscations to be a sharp blow against the German right-wing militants. This, however, remained to be seen as many of the members began to filter into other groups or set up a new organization under a new name. Although the monies and other paraphernalia were taken, the neo-Nazis seemed to be motivated strongly enough to continually start over after a brush with the police.

Neo-Nazi activities seemed to diminish precipitously during the latter part of 1994. There were cases of the displaced militant groups attempting to coalesce into larger organizations. For example, in Bavaria during late December, right-wing extremists, mostly identified as neo-Nazis, gathered in Marzling, a small town north of Munich, to hold a winter solstice bonfire. Approximately 160 extremists gathered in the local tavern close to a wooded area that included a large clearing in which the participants had piled logs ten feet high for their bonfire. Before the crowd could venture forward into the clearing, police raided the site and prohibited the militants from pursuing their evening entertainment.

Fittingly, December was also the month that Ewald Althans, a twenty-eight-year-old German thought by some to be the most notorious neo-Nazi during 1994, was convicted of inciting racial hatred by denying that the Holocaust had in fact occurred. The verdict supported the alleged acts of incitement, spreading banned neo-Nazi propaganda, and offending the memory of the dead. Althans then was sentenced to eighteen months in prison. This case was important in that not only was an individual found guilty of expressing his opinions in contravention to the norm expected in modern German society, but he was sentenced under the new laws.

By the end of 1994 the official web was tightening around the right-wing militant movement, taking away much of the rhetorical "power" exhibited by this movement since unification. Police officials and government agencies dealing with domestic security issues were becoming acutely aware of the signs that many of the heretofore seemingly quasi-dangerous neo-Nazi groups were drifting towards coalescing into a single, frightening movement that could very well shake the foundations of the democratic order in unified Germany.

NOTES

1. Ernst Zündel, a fifty-six-year-old professed neo-Nazi, is a well-known Holocaust denier. He owns and operates the Samisdat Publishing Company in Toronto, Canada, which is renowned for being one of the world's biggest suppliers of neo-Nazi and anti-Semitic propaganda. Through his contacts, Zündel was able to spread his opinions via books and videotapes, and on the computer Internet. From 1993 to early 1995, he shipped a weekly program entitled "Another Voice For Freedom" to radio and television stations throughout the United States. His venomous racial attacks and insistence that the Holocaust was a figment of western political rhetoric led many broadcasting companies to discontinue the weekly shows, including stations in Denver, Colorado; Lancaster, Pennsylvania; Nashville, Tennessee; and El Paso, Texas. This did not deter Ernst Zündel. He then brought suit in federal court to force approval for allowing his weekly program on the cable network. He was determined to disseminate his views of the Holocaust throughout the United States, hoping to obtain additional converts to his twisted perspective of history.

2. Michael Fox, "German Neo-Nazis Spread Message By Phone," *The Stars and Stripes* (August 27, 1994), 4.

3. Ibid.

4. Ibid.

5. Ibid.

6. *The Stars and Stripes* (September 3, 1994).

7. Jörg Friedrich, *Die Kalte Amnestie* (Munich: C.H. Beck, 1993), 45.

8. "Germans Outlaw Neo-Nazi Group," *The Stars and Stripes* (November 12, 1994).

8

International Cooperation

Jews are a plague. They have worms inside and these worms must be killed.
—Gary R. Lauck, *NS Kampfruf*, "Neo-Nazi Gets Last
Extradition Hearing," *The Stars and Stripes*, August 23, 1995

The German government's crackdown on right-wing extremists during late 1993 and through 1994 forced many neo-Nazis to consider alternative locations for their operations. The more sophisticated groups looked to Denmark as being the haven from increasing "persecution." Denmark's traditional liberalism allowing personal freedom of speech far beyond its European neighbors provided the perfect location for the continuance of the European neo-Nazi movement. The number of younger avowed neo-Nazis who were forced to leave Germany increased as the police honed in on the separate organizations and their leaders.

Waiting to accept these new immigrants were those Fascists who had long been in Denmark providing financial and moral support to their counterparts in Germany. Most infamous of these supporters was the ex-SS officer, Thies Christophersen, a seventy-four-year-old German who had lived in Denmark since 1986 and was an avid propagandist for the neo-Nazis. Christophersen became a "father" figure for many young right-wing militants. He provided financial support and insured that traveling militants had a place to stay while in Denmark. In July 1994, German officials requested that a twenty-three-year-old German charged with aggravated assault in Germany be extradited from Denmark;

the Danish police arrested the young man in Thies Christophersen's home. Even Denmark was becoming less desirable for the right-wing. For three months, Christophersen's residence was surrounded by approximately 1,500 anti-Nazi Danes who chanted "we shall have your hide."[1] Finally, complaining that he had been subjected to psychological terror, Thies Christophersen fled Denmark in late 1994.

German pressures to root out the most notable neo-Nazis who were being sought for specific crimes indicated a stronger resolution on the part of the government in Bonn to eradicate right-wing militancy in late 1994. Working with officials in adjoining countries, German officials forced the militants underground, making it increasingly difficult for neo-Nazis and skinheads to openly flaunt their extremism. The result of these methods was to be tested with a German effort to have an avowed neo-Nazi leader from the United States detained and sent to Germany for trial. Danish authorities played a key role in this international effort to take this infamous neo-Nazi out of circulation.

This American neo-Nazi set the precedence for closer international cooperation by actually forcing the re-interpretation of Danish law concerning extremism. Gary R. Lauck, age forty-one, was a familiar name among European neo-Nazis. For over twenty years, this self-proclaimed leader of the American neo-Nazi group, National Socialist German Worker's Party-Overseas Organization (NSDAP-OA), was the main source of neo-Nazi propaganda and literature for German right-wing militants. His newspaper, *NS Kampfruf* (*National Socialist Battle Cry*), was explicitly anti-Semitic and was specifically designed to support the old Nazi ideology. Through this printed forum, Lauck provided invidious articles attacking Jews and other minorities that he claimed were bad for society. Included with the short essays were numerous advertisements for obtaining more of his propaganda and Nazi-oriented items. As if this was not inflammatory enough, Lauck published security tips in the German editions that provided insights from his twenty years of experience into ways to smuggle propaganda into Germany. During a telephone interview held in early 1994, he claimed that he was equipping the German neo-Nazis with these propaganda materials because it was the same as supplying weapons for their crusade.

For years the German government had been trying to stop this flow of materials into Germany. Pressure on U.S. officials to deal with Lauck proved ineffective, since he had broken no laws in the United States. Gary Lauck was a wanted man only in Germany. Ironically, Lauck did fly into Berlin and met with Michael Kühnen and Christian Worch in 1990.[2] He was filmed leaving the airport being escorted by these two well-known neo-Nazis without incident. Upon becoming public in 1993, this film material only infuriated the German police more, making Lauck's opportunities of returning to Germany almost non-existent.

In order to stop Gary Lauck's propaganda efforts in Germany, it took an extradition request to a neighboring nation and constant perseverance that finally paid off. Lauck flew to Denmark in March 1995 to attend a regional neo-Nazi conference. There were suggestions that he planned to immigrate to Denmark seeking asylum, because of his fear that the Federal Bureau of Investigation (FBI) may have been after him for his right-wing activities in the United States and the inflammatory materials he was shipping overseas. Ingo Hasselbach, the National Alternative neo-Nazi leader who became a state witness, indicated that the bombing in Oklahoma City of the Alfred P. Murrah Federal Building led to FBI cooperation with Germany to have Lauck extradited.[3] Gary Lauck delighted in calling the United States the "Jew-nited" States.[4] He found the United States a useful place to live because of the few restrictions on weapons ownership and political speech.

On March 20, 1995, Danish police arrested Lauck, two weeks after his arrival, following testimony provided by Hasselbach and a request for his extradition to Germany for distributing anti-Semitic propaganda to German Nationals.[5] He was detained in Roskilde, Denmark, a small town twenty-five miles west of Copenhagen, until a decision could be reached on whether or not to meet the extradition request.

In his initial hearing, Gary Lauck claimed that his publications were "political and nonviolent," and included only "theoretical studies." The Danish prosecutor Anders Leunet countered this argument by using Lauck's own description of his role in the neo-Nazi movement, that of being the leading figure of "an international and professional propaganda organization" referred to as the NSDAP-OA, and which was banned in Germany in 1974. Lauck's defense attorney, Erik Liisborg, argued that Gary Lauck had not broken any Danish or U.S. laws, and therefore should be released. His legal argument was predicated on the foundation of Danish extradition law, which stated that a person could only be extradited to another country if their activities were illegal in Denmark.

The Lauck case became an important symbol for right-wing militant groups, as well as the nations in Europe that were facing increased mobilization of the neo-Nazi movement. Fifteen neo-Nazis kept a peaceful, but very visible, vigil outside the court building during the proceedings. The German government was constantly pressuring the Danes to extradite the American neo-Nazi. The Germans accused Lauck of distributing illegal propaganda and Nazi symbols, incitement, encouraging racial hatred, and belonging to a criminal group. German law could potentially invoke a jail sentence of up to fourteen years if

Lauck was convicted in Germany.

In the first legal maneuvering, the Danish Justice Department approved the extradition, forcing Lauck to appeal to the court system. His attorney once again argued that Lauck had not violated Danish law. This appeal was denied when the lower court found that Danish authorities could extradite because Lauck's publication activities were, in fact, considered illegal in Denmark. Lauck was rapidly losing his battle against being sent to Germany for trial. This was proving to be an unusual example of international law, where an American citizen visiting a foreign nation was detained and then would be transferred to a third country for trial. The complexity of this effort was simplified primarily because of the abhorrence that all three nations felt concerning the activities of this one man.

By law, Lauck was offered one more chance to appeal his extradition. In August 1995, the prosecutor, Kasper Linkis, argued that Lauck's material in his publications was, by Danish law, illegal because it contained "systematic use of grossly negative statements about Jews." He went on to quote Lauck's newspaper article that said "Jews are a plague. They have worms inside and these worms must be killed." The court interpreted this statement as an order to the neo-Nazis to kill Jews. On August 24, 1995, Denmark's highest court, with Chief Judge Marie-Louise Andreasen presiding, rejected Lauck's argument that he was working for political change and approved the legality of extradition to Germany. The judge ruled definitively that Lauck's statement did violate Denmark's law on racism.

On September 5, 1995, Gary R. Lauck was transferred from Roskilde, Denmark, to Hamburg, Germany, to await trial. He, however, was not the only "catch" that German authorities made during the Summer of 1995. In an associated case, a sixty-eight-year-old German-born American, Hans Schmidt of Pensacola, Florida, was arrested in Germany while on vacation. He was jailed for inciting racial hatred through his published newsletter, which he was distributing during his German visit. This particular edition of the newspaper denied that the Nazis slaughtered Jews during World War II and referred to the Jews as "contamination." Schmidt came under the same law as Lauck and faced the same potential five year prison sentence if convicted in the German courts.

The importance of these two cases highlighted the growing frustrations in Germany. For years, neo-Nazis and right-wing extremists outside of Germany had fueled the fires of young discontents within German borders. German efforts to obtain support of foreign governments in curbing these activities were never productive, particularly with the United States. The German government literally declared war on the neo-Nazis during the latter part of 1994 and into 1995. This included insuring that outsiders were susceptible to the judicial system that was attempting to eradicate the right-wing movement. The efforts in the Lauck and Schmidt cases showed a sincere desire on Germany's part to pursue those who espoused the Nazi ideology that was so antithetic to Germany's democratic principles. This required cutting off the many tentacles of the growing international neo-Nazi movement by bringing charges against not only Germans, but against those outside of Germany. Targeted were those who traditionally provided fuel for the fires of discontent and violence that right-wing militants wielded for years before unification and more viciously following unification of the two Germanies. Following Lauck's arrest, German police conducted a major operation, called "Atlantik II," in which they raided right-wing militant cells all over Germany.[6] A total of eighty-four apartments were searched. Links between right-wing groups were broken, and vast amounts of propaganda and terrorist equipment were seized.

It became blatantly obvious, following the decisions in Denmark, that neo-Nazis in Europe or from the United States could not be guaranteed an open sanctuary on Danish territory. This was an indication that nations familiar with the Nazi past were increasingly more supportive when other nations were attempting to control the growing neo-Nazi movement. The neo-Nazi movement looked to Sweden as the next possible sanctuary. Jürgen Rieger, a Hamburg lawyer known for defending top neo-Nazis, bought an eighteenth-century Swedish manor on 1,600 acres in order to develop a new neo-Nazi colony.[7]

At the end of 1994, it appeared that the neo-Nazi movement was on a constant declination path. Although there were still documented right-wing activities, the incidents were far fewer than at any time since unification. German officials no longer viewed these extremists as a fringe element that was largely a bother rather than a danger. Anti-neo-Nazi programs played a key role in forcing many of the militant leaders into hiding and a number into jails for periods of two to five years. Multinational efforts to isolate and diminish the efforts of the neo-Nazis were becoming more effective. And yet, the cancer of right-wing extremism, with its National Socialist baggage, remained in the fabric of German society. In fact, right-wing fascist groups, which often were organized along the ideological basis of the German Nazi past, flourished in ever more diverse areas. Right-wing extremism and militancy grew more influential in lands that only four years earlier were under the tight control of the Communist Party, the defunct Soviet Union and its client states. Even in the United States, where white supremacists used symbols and ideology of the abhorrent Nazis, the growing militancy of the right-wing resulted in bombings in north Idaho; killings in California, Colorado, and Oregon; and the growth of paramilitary organizations that were anti-government and often racist. White supremacist groups in the United States were linked to twenty murders in 1990, thirteen more than in 1989.[8] Anti-Semitic activities showed an increase from 489 in 1980 to 1,685 in 1990.[9] Estimates are that there are over 300 of these groups in the United States with approximately 25,000 members.

By early 1995, German government officials still estimated that there were at least 40,000 neo-Nazis in Germany. Of those, only a small hard-core number were still active within the German borders and in the adjoining lands. From 1990 to the end of 1994, German neo-Nazis and their skinhead militia were credited with the murders of thirty-one people. During this time, over 5,000 attacks were perpetrated on immigrants and German nationals alike. Although the number of beatings seemed to be fewer in 1995, there were still incidents of neo-Nazi violence. In what appeared to officials to be copycat violence, a string of mail bombings occurred in Germany just after the Oklahoma City bombing. During the Spring of 1995, four Gypsies were killed by a pipe bomb. Over the summer months, a liberal German politician and a talk-show host received mail bombs. And in the Fall of 1995, in Austria, a Syrian-born doctor and a refugee-relief worker were severely injured by separate mail bomb attacks.

On May 25, 1995, neo-Nazis beat to death a twenty-four year old man while he was walking in the woods during his holiday vacation. Police estimated that as many as fifteen men attacked the victim with baseball bats, beating him so badly that he died within days. This vicious attack occurred near the city of Chemnitz, not far from the eastern German city of Dresden in the state of Sachsen.

In August 1995, neo-Nazis demonstrated in Diksmuide, Belgium. Police broke up the parade after the right-wing militants attacked the local police station. Over 200 foreign activists, mostly German, were expelled from Belgium following this violent demonstration.

The German neo-Nazis respected no borders when it came to their activities and rhetoric. Police blotters all over northern Europe identified the average violent neo-Nazi as traditionally male (95.3 percent) and over one-half of those were less than twenty-one years old (67 percent). In general, those who were involved in violence from 1990 to 1995 were unemployed and relatively uneducated. Alcohol was found to have been involved in the majority of violent activities conducted by these right-wing thugs.

At the end of 1994 and in early 1995, the German government, in conjunction with *Länder* governments, banned an additional number of the better known neo-Nazi organizations in Germany. The outlawing of the Viking Youth in November 1994 was only the beginning of the effort to exclude the right-wing extremists from German society. In December, four more neo-Nazi groups were banned. Government officials considered these groups to be the most virulent right-wing militants in Germany. The groups included the German Nationalists (DN), the Direct Action group in Central Germany, the NPD's youth organization, JN (Youth Nationalists), and the *Hilfsorganisation für Nationale Politische Gefangenen und deren Aneghörige, E.V.* (Assistance Organization for National Political Prisoners and Their Family Members, Registered Association), commonly referred to as the HNG. This organization originally was designed to assist fellow neo-Nazis by working under the guise of what they called "protecting national political prisoners."

The HNG was founded in 1979, and by 1994 it included over 200 members in Germany. In August 1991, Ursula Müller, wife of the well-known neo-Nazi Curt Müller, was elected president of the organization. The Müllers long had been involved in the neo-Nazi movement. They lived in Mainz-Gonsenheim, in the Rheinland-Pfalz region, and Curt was the leader of a small group called *Neonazikreis um Curt Müller*. This group organized meetings to which neo-Nazis from all over Germany would congregate at the Müller residence.

The government's bans were a sharp attack on the most radical neo-Nazi organizations in Germany. The next group to be banned was a key blow to the right-wing movement. On February 24, 1995, the German Ministry of the Interior finally outlawed the venerable neo-Nazi group, the Free German Worker's Party (FAP). The FAP was first founded in 1979 and quickly became one of the most militant neo-Nazi groups. Their activities were fairly innocuous until 1984, when right-wing radicals from the banned ANS/NA (National Socialist Action Front/National Activists) infiltrated the group, making the entire organization far more militant. By 1993, the FAP boasted over 430 hard-core members led by Friedhelm Busse. This particular neo-Nazi organization participated in numerous state, federal, and European Union elections prior to 1989. After 1989, the FAP appeared to lose interest in the political process and began leaning more heavily towards militancy. This generated more interest on the part of the police. The Ministry of the Interior, citing that their authority to ban the FAP came from the Basic Law, ruled against the neo-Nazi organization on the grounds that FAP activities were "directed against the constitutional order of Germany." This decision was predicated on the basis that the FAP was not considered a political party, which only could be banned by constitutional courts. This ruling authorized the Ministry of the Interior to decide on a ban without having to go through the time-consuming court system. At the direction of the Minister of the Interior's policing agency, *Verfassungsschutz* (Office for the Protection of the Constitution), police raided the FAP offices. They seized weapons, propaganda, fax machines, membership lists, and financial records. Interestingly, the FAP appeared to be ready for the raids. Although these raids were supposedly kept secret, some of the FAP membership officially resigned and numerous documents were shredded just prior to the police actions.

Manfred Kanther, the Interior Minister, compared the FAP to the NSDAP. He charged the organization with engaging in anti-Semitic and xenophobic agitation and slandering the democratic institutions of Germany. He commented that the FAP leaders repeatedly stated the desire to assume power in Germany and eliminate political opponents. The Minister also claimed that this neo-Nazi group maintained close contacts with right-wing extremist organizations throughout Europe and abroad. The final banning of this organization was considered to be a major blow to the neo-Nazi movement in Germany.

Also in early 1995, the Minister of the Interior for the state government of Hamburg banned the local *Nationale Liste* (NL) organization. This neo-Nazi group was founded in 1989 from supporters of the banned ANS/NA cell in Hamburg. The thirty known members considered themselves to be the cadre of a potentially large neo-Nazi organization. Their goal was to consolidate the right-wing militants throughout Germany under the leadership of Christian Worch by using an information networking system. As far as their opponents were concerned, the NL used ample intimidation to strike fear among those who questioned or opposed the validity of the movement. Following the Hamburg Minister of the Interior's decision to officially ban the NL, police raids were conducted to collect evidence of the group's activities and membership.

The official efforts to eliminate the organizational structures of the most notable neo-Nazi groups at both the state and federal levels were designed to inhibit the growth of right-wing extremism in Germany. By interpreting the laws to exclude the right-wing neo-Nazis from the legal category of political organizations, it made it far easier to ban these groups quickly without having to resort to lengthy judicial proceedings. By being more precise in the definition of a political party, government officials at all levels had far more flexibility to combat neo-Nazism. The extremists no longer could use the more protected status simply by registering as a political party and participating marginally in local and federal elections.

There was, however, at least one major problem associated with the principle of banning radical groups. Invariably, once a group was banned, the leaders and membership quickly assumed a new name and continued to function as before, albeit with more care and tending to go further underground, making it even more difficult for officials to track their activities. Even the efforts to adjudicate against the leaders often resulted in fairly short sentences, often making this individual a martyr in the eyes of his followers. Although a number of these leaders were incarcerated for different periods of time ranging from a few months to up to five years, there was always someone else to step in and continue leading the activities of the different groups.

Another product of the government efforts to "cut off the head" of the neo-Nazi movement was the inevitable combining of right-wing forces for survivability. The consolidation of the international neo-Nazi movement was a direct result of pressures against the heretofore individual neo-Nazi and skinhead groups that were scattered throughout eastern and western Germany, as well as in adjoining countries. It became apparent to many in the right-wing movement that survival depended upon joining their resources.

NOTES

1. Ingo Hasselbach, "How Nazis Are Made," *The New Yorker* (January 8, 1996), 55.

2. Michael Schmidt, Producer/Director, *Wahrheit Macht Frei*, a film produced in October 1991.

3. Hasselbach, 55.

4. Hasselbach, 47.

5. Ibid., 55.

6. Ibid.

7. Ibid.

8. Carol J. Castaneda, "Hate Crimes And Killings Are On The Rise," *USA Today* (September 6, 1991), 3A.

9. Ibid.

9

The "Miracle"

[The] German people have achieved their unity.
—German Basic Law, Amended 1990

Within weeks following the official day of German unification, the Germans'
enthusiasm for once again having a whole nation began to wane and doubt began
to creep in as to the advisability of such a momentous decision. Germans from
both sides of the newly unified nation began to question the premises that
brought two such different societies together into a single sovereign economic
unit.

Five years later, after weathering the difficulties associated with the social and
economic adjustments, a good many Germans felt a certain accomplishment for
having overcome what seemed the impossible. Yes, there were still the
pessimists and the critics. This, however, did not deter the German leaders who
spoke of an economic and political miracle in just a short five years.

Government and public announcements painted a very positive picture of
unified Germany in 1995. In support of these arguments, statisticians pointed
out that unemployment in April 1995 was down to 9.4 percent overall. In the
western *Länder*, this percentage reflected a reasonable 8.3 percent. The miracle
appeared to be in the eastern states, where only five years earlier unemployment
hovered around 50 percent and was now touted to be 13.9 percent. Bernhard
Jagoda, Head of the German Labor Office, provided the figure that only
3,604,692 were unemployed throughout unified Germany in the Spring of

1995.[1]

The costs of unification, a major fear for many Germans in the West, leveled off during 1994 and early 1995. Coming in below original estimates, the $700 billion spent on welfare and public works for stability in the East was considered an investment well made.[2] Bonn's anticipation to spend at least $70 billion annually to continue subsidizing the development in the eastern five states and East Berlin for another decade was considered by the politicians as more than palatable. It appeared that indeed, on the surface at least, this was a "miracle" in this decade, with seemingly insurmountable obstacles overcome by sheer energy and sufficient resources.

On the other hand, a question still lingered as to the real state of the union. A sense of discouragement appeared to continue in the populations of both East and West Germany. Many easterners complained that unification was too much a one-way street. They vocalized the impression that western German business-men were making the major decisions in the East. These people saw the results being that the eastern employees and businessmen were the primary economic casualties in this arrangement.

The Germans in the five eastern states, in many cases, still felt that a wall existed between the East and West. This wall was no longer the physical barrier that the Berlin Wall represented, but it was an emotional wall that was almost as effective in keeping the sides apart. Having been under Communist rule for so many years, many easterners felt uncomfortable with the decline of what they saw as the community and family virtues associated with the Communist system, and being replaced with a society that stressed money and self. Surveys conducted in 1994 indicated that over one-half of the interviewed easterners saw themselves as better off than in 1989, mostly because of the West's generous social safety net, however, over two-thirds said that capitalism was incompatible with humanness. Hilmar Schneider, an economist with the Institute for Economic Research located in the eastern city of Halle, summed up this dichotomy by saying that "[it is] difficult for West Germans to understand that even though East Germans are doing very well materially, many are not that well emotionally."[3]

The unemployment figures seemed to be within reasonable parameters, and yet the right-wing extremists continued to attract supporters. Critics indicated a possible fallacy in the government's interpretation of the statistics. They argued that the use of part-time employment in calculating the employment and retraining programs rate tended to skew the findings, particularly in the eastern regions. Including part-time employment and retraining as true employment, the critics insisted, was not really gainful employment that provided for the standard of living needed to support a family. They went on to say that the government's inclusion of these statistics provided a false impression of the actual unemployment rate. In reviewing the data, although the unemployment in the East appeared to be reasonable, the fact remained that one in four employable persons in the eastern states were unemployed and could not find work. Tens of thousands were in retraining programs, government-created jobs, or took early retirement. In 1991, over ninety-seven percent of women between twenty-five and thirty-four years of age still held jobs. By 1995, only sixty percent of these women still had employment.

The 16 million East Germans constitute close to 20 percent of the total German population. Statistics in 1995 showed that this group accounted for 10.4 percent of the total national gross domestic product. Although this was an increase from 7.2 percent in 1991, evidently many easterners did not agree that the economic miracle in Germany had spread across the nation evenly. Many residents in the eastern *Länder* still felt that they were second class citizens and that the westerners were the actual recipients of the benefits of economic growth. The average easterner toiled 1,701 hours in 1994, whereas the average westerner worked 1,584 hours.[4] In the East, approximately 19.9 percent of the household income was spent on housing and utilities. Those in the West spent, on an average, 28.7 percent on the same requirements. Materially, the differences found in 1994 also reflected the disparity between the regions. States in the East had thirty-four telephone lines per 100 homes in comparison to fifty-one per 100 in the west. There were only six percent of the homes in the East with dishwashers, in contrast to thirty-nine percent in the western homes; sixty-seven percent of the easterners owned cars, whereas seventy-five percent owned automobiles in the West. There is no doubt that these statistics were more positive for the eastern states than only a short five years earlier. This, however, does not explain why the richest municipality in the East was still poorer than the poorest municipality in the West.

In addition, the East Germans were still very much under-represented in Germany's political and government circles, leaving the impression that easterners were still not as acceptable as their western brethren. German unification was an important issue for Willy Brandt during the Cold War. He insisted that "what belongs together should grow together," referring to the two Germanies. In 1995, this concept was modified to account for the unifying of two very distinct and often alien cultures that would take time to truly grow together. This was best said by Thomas Flierl, head of the Cultural Office, when he commented that, "One has to live together. But grow together?"[5]

It is apparent that the East and West Germans began the long road to final reconciliation and eventual solidification of a truly German nation. Kohl's government developed a number of options over the past five years to alleviate problems and resolve issues quickly. Upon beginning his new four year term as chancellor, Helmut Kohl set goals to deal with the difficult questions regarding social needs versus federal resources. Costs skyrocketed during the 1980s and immediately following unification. His efforts were designed to gain control of the spiraling costs that impacted unification and the quality of life for his constituents.

Kohl's platform included two major concepts that directly impacted on the social strata of Germans. First, he recommended cutting aid to unemployed people who refused jobs. This, however, appeared to impact most heavily on the eastern population, where jobs were scarce and officials tended to consider part-time as equal to full-time. Second, he addressed the issue of foreigners and German citizenship. As a potential settlement between the 6.9 million foreigners in Germany and the German population that feared the dilution of their society by outsiders, he suggested that foreign immigrants' children born in Germany be granted temporary dual citizenship. This was caveated by requiring the parents to have lived in Germany for at least ten years. Although this sounded like a magnanimous position in support of the foreign community, in fact this only affected approximately 9,000 people.[6] Kohl's position, although well intentioned, provided grist for the right-wing. These extremists saw this change in the policies that seemed to support asylum seekers and immigrants as detrimental to modern German society and the future of Germany.

The German parliament's response to the right-wing fears of open foreign immigration and continued stress on German economic and societal foundations was to amend the Basic Law. Although initially drafted as a temporary framework for a future constitution (once Germany was unified), this document became the primary law of the land following formal unification. It was upgraded to state that, with the accession of the defunct German Democratic Republic, the "German people have achieved their unity." On October 3, 1990, the Basic Law was validated for the entire unified Germany, providing a national, applicable law.

Of direct interest to the right-wing was the amendment to the Basic Law, approved in 1993, that impacted on the issue of asylum. Article 16a of the Basic Law modified the asylum procedures without violating the principle that "anyone persecuted on political grounds has the right of asylum" [in Germany]. The new Article was designed to placate the right-wing fears that asylum seekers were diluting the German social system and bankrupting the support program. By more clearly defining the recipients, the government restricted the open-ended movement of immigrants into Germany who then were eligible for financial help. The new wording in the Basic Law clearly stated that foreign nationals from Economic Community (EC) countries or from "safe Third Countries" could not "invoke the right of asylum, nor [can they] remain in the country [Germany] on a temporary basis." In addition, the new Article specifically broached the subject of support payment fraud by including a statement which insured that social benefits were limited to a single claim rather than the often practiced multiple claims from nucleus and extended families.

The Basic Law, utilizing the new Article 16a, still guaranteed protection from political persecution as a basic individual right. The primary premise of the change was focused on insuring that truly persecuted individuals, those immigrating on political grounds, were afforded protection. Results of the change were quickly realized. In 1989, a recorded 121,318 foreigners sought asylum protection in Germany. During 1991, this number increased to 256,112 and by 1992, the applications for asylum rose to 438,191. From January through June 1993, asylum seekers continued to enter Germany in record numbers. The new Asylum Law went into effect on July 1, 1993. This precipitated a significant decrease in the number of immigrants requesting formal asylum. Applications dropped to less than five percent of the number prior to the new law. This change was a coup for the government in response to the right-wing criticism over the previous years.

Neo-Nazis long flaunted the government's apparent open-door asylum policies. This was an issue that the extremists used without mercy in supporting their attacks against non-Germans. Now, the right-wing's ability to argue that foreigners were overwhelming Germany was becoming a less viable diatribe for arousing heated support in unified Germany. (See Table 9.1.)

Since its inception, the Basic Law provided a legal means to deal with organizations within Germany that endangered the governmental democratic structures. This safeguarding of the democratic system was defined in the original Basic Law as "protection of the Constitution," which was considered a fundamental right of the democratically elected government. This protection insured that the laws could not be usurped in the same way that Hitler was able to come to power and wield dictatorial powers that overwhelmed the tenuous principles of the Weimar Republic. The Basic Law protection was ensured by authorizing state and federal authorities information collected about extremists, their activities, and other developments that constituted a possible threat to national security. In addition, these governmental agencies were allowed to evaluate and store this information for the central and state governments, ministries, and courts. Critics of this portion of the Basic Law argued that this was an invasion of basic individual rights. This particular portion of the law, however, was written as a result of the Nazi experience and was felt to be a small price to pay for the protection against subversion and terrorism.

Efforts to combat right-wing extremism in Germany since unification impacted, but did not eradicate, the neo-Nazis or their supporters. Government efforts, through legislation, to defuse the neo-Nazi movement had mixed results. Changing asylum laws took away a major political issue for the right-wing, but did not seem to hinder the militants who still saw thousands of foreigners in Germany. The government's seemingly favorite means of dealing with the neo-Nazis, banning their organizations, seemed to be somewhat ineffective. On the one hand, officials were given the opportunity to raid homes and offices of the offenders, thereby confiscating large quantities of weapons, communications equipment, propaganda, and illegal materials. Yet, on the other hand, these groups dissolved on one day and within a short period of time re-emerged as the same organization, but with a new name. In addition, these groups often combined with other banned groups, beginning the process of amalgamating into a far more potent militant organization.

TABLE 9.1
Foreign Nationals In Germany (1995)

Turks	1,855,000
Yugoslav Refugees	Approx 1,000,000
Italians	558,000
Greeks	346,000
Poles	286,000
Austrians	185,000
Rumanians	167,000
Spaniards	134,000
Vietnamese	86,000
Moroccans	80,000
Lebanese	53,000
Sri Lankans	44,000
Afghans	42,000
Indians	36,000

60 percent have lived in Germany over ten years and two-thirds of foreign children were born in Germany.

Dealing with the neo-Nazi problem became a difficult and dangerous effort. The continued presence of this right-wing extremism in Germany, although fairly inconsequential, except to the victims and their families, remained an interesting phenomenon for those who watched the growth of modern Germany into a strong and viable democracy. One wonders if this is a cyclical movement that will dissipate with the strengthening of unified Germany's economic and political foundations, or is there something in the psyche of the German people that continues to provide support for such nationalist radicalism?

NOTES

1. "Number of Jobless Declines In Germany," *The Stars and Stripes* (May 15, 1995).

2. Frank Bajak, "Still Divided," *The Stars and Stripes* (October 9, 1995), 18.

3. Ibid., 19.

4. Ibid.

5. Ibid.

6. "Kohl To Push Welfare Cuts, Less Red Tape," *The Stars and Stripes* (January 12, 1994).

10

Epilogue

Five years after unification it is readily apparent that there are still a number of young people in Germany who have forgotten or have never learned about the history of the Third Reich. These youth, supported by a few elders who have carried the banner of the Nazi ideology, continue to propagate the vicious and dangerous rhetoric of the National Socialist Worker's Party, mixed with their own concept of modern Germany. They still hate, or misunderstand, and fear foreigners, Jews, and the principles of democracy. Amelie Mummendey, a professor of psychology at the University of Münster, found that the right-wing extremists generally assume that their behavior is accepted with a certain amount of sympathy among other Germans.[1] She went on to recommend methods of overcoming this perception, urging Germans to "deny social support of xenophobic elements, highlight foreigners' positive characteristics, and take an active interest in foreigners' problems and cultural diversities."[2]

Other experts suggested that the German "lack of civic courage" when dealing with the neo-Nazis was a result of indifference, prejudice, and anonymity in society, which lead to German indifference.[3] Hermann Lutz, the German Police Union Chairman, argued that "citizens who look away are partly responsible for the spread of violence."[4] He went on to say that police were also part of the problem when they react too harshly or too weakly, thereby convincing people that the police are "arbitrary."

As if to clarify that the right-wing militants are still active, the German People's Union, a known politically oriented neo-Nazi organization, held an annual rally in September 1995. Two thousand and five hundred right-wing extremists, principally made up of neo-Nazis throughout Germany, held a joint rally in the German town of Passau, just on the border with Austria. Passau officials had been able to delay the meeting for months by refusing the group's repeated requests to hold the activities in their vicinity. This, however, did not deter the final gathering on that early Fall day at the end of September.

Police raided the activities and arrested twenty-two people for illegal possession of weapons, displaying banned symbols, and committing other crimes during the annual rally. The arrests were not made easily. Several clashes occurred between the participant extremists and the police. As was the case so many times before, all of those who were arrested, except five, were released by the next day.

Eradication of the neo-Nazis is a formidable job. Individual rights associated with democracies make it even more difficult unless the laws are specifically broken. Only recently have nations that have these extremists within their borders begun to coordinate efforts to preclude the spread of the neo-Nazi poison. Punishment is becoming more stringent as the militants become more brutal. Government actions are more focused, yet the groups seem to survive.

Public education to the excesses and abuses of these groups is probably the most effective means of combatting this movement. Punishment for crimes against others should be sufficient to deter participation. International efforts must be coordinated to break the ties between the different militant groups and to insure that there is no safe haven for such groups that use hate and intimidation as a cornerstone of their philosophy. These militant activists are enamored with Hitler's short tenure as a dictator in Central Europe. They have shown the propensity to be active in the overt political scene and to work in the covert arena using terrorism. They are most dangerous as a propaganda machine that feeds off of fear and unhappiness. These groups exist throughout Europe and North America, and right-wing extremist mutations can be found around the world. There is little doubt that they are a valid danger to democratic societies and principles.

NOTES

1. "Indifference Encourages Rightist Thugs, Experts Say," *The Stars and Stripes* (May 29, 1994), 8.
2. Ibid.
3. Ibid.
4. Ibid.

Selected Bibliography

Andresen, Karen. "Der Hässliche Deutsche." *Der Stern Magazine,* February 1989, 2.

Assheuer, Thomas and Hans Sarkowicz. *Rechtsradikale In Deutschland.* Munich: Verlag C. H. Beck, 1992.

Baensch, Torsten. *Jugendlichen Raum Lassen?* Hamburg: Lütcke & Wulff, 1992.

Bajak, Frank. "Still Divided." *The Stars and Stripes,* October 9, 1995.

Benjamin, Daniel. "Cracking Down On The Right." *Time,* December 14, 1992, 43-45.

Binder, David. "Violence By Skinheads Startling East Germans." *The New York Times,* August 21, 1990, Section A2/page 1.

Böhme, Erich. "Der Rock rutscht hoch." *Der Spiegel,* February 6, 1989, 6.

Breslau, Karen. "Germany's Chaotic Spring." *Newsweek,* May 11, 1992, 20.

Bundesminister des Innern. *Terroristen In Kampf Gegen Recht und Menschen würde.* Bonn: Graphische Betriebe, 1992.

_____. *Verfassungsschutzbericht, 1987, 1988, 1989, 1990, 1991, 1992, 1993, 1994.* Bonn: Graphische Betriebe.

Castenada, Carol J. "Hate Crimes And Killings Are On The Rise." *USA Today,* September 6, 1991, 3A.

Dayton Daily News (Ohio). "Violence, Death Mar German's Victory Rights," July 10, 1990, 4A.

Der Spiegel Magazine. "Augen Im Hinterkopf," August 1993, 35-38.

_____. "Den Ruf Lädiert," August 1994.

_____. "Köpfe Rollen," July 1993, 26-27.

_____. "Reisiges Gelächter," August 1993, 108-109.

_____. "Spiel Mir Das Lied," July 1993, 47 & 52.

Der Stern Magazine. "Gewalt Macht Spass," November 11, 1993, 254-255.

_____. "Neo-Nazis," November 11, 1993, 18-22.

_____. "Nuremberg II," August 19, 1995, 35.

The Economist. "Shadows In The East," June 23, 1990, 43.

_____. "Variegated Winners, Red-Green Losers," December 8, 1990, 56-58.

The European. "Arrests Stem Nazi Tribute To Hess," August 1994.

Farin, Klaus and Eberhard Seidel-Pielen. *Skinheads.* Munich: Verlag C. H. Beck, 1993.

Fox, Michael. "German Neo-Nazis Spread Message By Phone." *The Stars and Stripes,* August 27, 1994, 12.

Frankfurter Rundschau. "Public Reactions To Mölln Murders," November 24, 1992.

Friedrich, Jörge. *Die Kalte Amnestie.* Munich: Verlag C. H. Beck, 1993.

Hasselbach, Ingo with Tom Reiss. "How Nazis Are Made." *The New Yorker,* January 8, 1996, 36-57.

Hugues, Pascale. "Bonn Flexes New Diplomatic Muscle." *World Press Review,* April 1992, 22-24.

Jarausch, Konrad H. *The Rush To German Unity.* New York: Oxford University Press, 1994.

Keilinger, Thomas. "East And West: United In Name, Not In Spirit." *World Press Review,* vol 38/no 6, June 1991, 20.

Kinzer, Stephen. "Hitler's Ascent Is Recalled With Sorrow By Germans." *The New York Times,* January 31, 1993, 10.

Koring, Paul. "Politics Of Hate Disturb A Wary Europe." *Pittsburgh Press* (Pennsylvania), November 31, 1991, B-1.

Kramer, Jane. "Neo-Nazis: A Chaos In The Head." *The New Yorker,* June 14, 1993, 52-70.

Leggewie, Claus. *Druck von Rechts Wohin triebt die Bundesrepublik?* Munich: Verlag C. H. Beck, 1993.

Lewis, Rand C. *A Nazi Legacy: Right-Wing Extremism In Postwar Germany.* New York: Praeger Publishing, 1991.

_____. "German Unification And Right-Wing Extremism." *Topic 44, New And Old Problems For A Unified Germany.* Washington, Pennsylvania: Washington and Jefferson College, 1993, 43-52.

McFeatters, Dale. "Unification An Economic Miracle." *The Stars and Stripes,* September 10, 1995.

Morshaeuser, Bodo. *Warten Auf Dem Führer.* Frankfurt am Main: Suhrkamp, 1993.

Newsweek. "Europe's New Right," April 27, 1992, 32-34.

The New York Review. "The German Revolution," December 21, 1989.

Pieciak, Wojciech. "The New Threat Of The Right," *World Press Review,* May 1992, 22-24.

Prince, Michael K. "Germany, Europe And The Dilemma Of Democratic Legitimization." *Aussen Politik.* Hamburg: Interpres Verlag, GmbH, 3-13.

Protzman, Ferdinand. "West Germany Must Pay To Play Unification Game." *Dayton Daily News* (Ohio), October 1, 1990.

Roth, Dieter. *"Die Republikaner:* The Rise and Fall Of A Far Right Protest P ar ty ." Paper presented at the 1990 annual meeting of the American Political Science Association, San Francisco, California, August 30-September 2, 1990.

The Stars and Stripes (European Edition). "Bavarian Police Prevent Neo-Nazi Bonfire," December 19, 1994.

_____. "Bonn Pushes Legislation To Curb Right-Wing Activity," May 12, 1994.

_____. "14 Escape Arson Attack On Refugees In Germany," November 15, 1993, 11.

_____. "German Police Accused Of Brutalizing Foreigners," May 17, 1995, 10.

_____. "Germans Outlaw Neo-Nazi Group," November 12, 1994.

_____. "Germany Likely To Support Bill To Ban 'Auschwitz Lie'," May 15, 1994, 12.

_____. "Indifference Encourages Rightist Thugs, Experts Say," May 28, 1994, 8.

_____. "Kohl To Push Welfare Cuts, Less Red Tape," January 15, 1994.

_____. "Neo-Nazi Gets Last Extradition Hearing," August 23, 1995.

_____. "Neo-Nazi Gets 18 Months For Hate Crime In Germany," December 17, 1994.

_____. "Neo-Nazis Sentenced," August 31, 1994.

_____. "Number Of Jobless Declines In Germany," May 15, 1995.

_____. "Punishment Urged For Neo-Nazis Who Rampaged At Buchenwald," August 12, 1994.

_____. "Spain Hunts Nazi General Who Rejected Holocaust," May 27, 1994.

_____. "U.S. Neo-Nazi Sent To Germany For Trial," September 7, 1995, 13.

U.S. News & World Report. "The Far Right Senses Opportunity," June 1, 1992, 44.

_____. "Down And Out At The Cabaret," June 1, 1992, 44.

_____. "The Shadow Of Their Swastika," June 15, 1992, 36-40.

The Week In Germany. "Bonn, GDR Sign Unification Treaty," September 7, 1990.

_____ "Election '90': A Solid Mandate For Kohl's Coalition," December 7, 1990.

_____. "Number Of Skinheads In Germany Estimated At 4,200," November 27, 1992, 1-2.

_____. "Three Turkish Residents Die In Right-Wing Attack: Bonn Speaks Of Outrage, Bitterness, And Sorrow," November 27, 1992, 1-3.

von Weizsäcker, Richard. "The Dignity Of Man Is Inviolable." *Statements and Speeches,* vol XV, no 17. New York: German Information Center, 1992.

Wilkerson, Paul. *The New Fascist.* London: Grant McIntyre Ltd., 1981. *World Press Review.* "The Violent Rise Of Hitler's New Youth," August 1991, 22-23.

Index

About the Author

RAND C. LEWIS, a retired U.S. Army officer, was Associate Professor at the Defense Institute of Security Assistance Management, Wright-Patterson AFB, Ohio and Professor of Military Science at Duquesne University. He spent several years living in Germany, where he wrote numerous articles dealing with right-wing militancy. He is also author of *A Nazi Legacy* (Praeger, 1993).